May I Kiss You?

A Candid Look at Dating, Communication, Respect, & Sexual Assault Awareness

Michael J. Domitrz

AWARENESS
PUBLICATIONS

Greenfield, Wisconsin

May I Kiss You? A Candid Look at Dating, Communication, Respect, & Sexual Assault Awareness, is a trademark of Domitrz & Associates LLC, Awareness Publications LLC, and Michael J. Domitrz, denoting a series of products that may include but are not limited to books, pocket cards, calendars, audio cassettes, videotapes, and compact discs (CDs).

Edited by: Carolyn Kott Washburne
Cover and text design by: Georgene Schreiner

ISBN: 978-0-9729282-0-5
Library of Congress Control Number: 2003103171

Printed in the United States of America
First Printing 2003
Fifth Printing 2008

12   11   10   9   8   7   6

Publisher's Cataloging-in-Publication Data
Domitrz, Michael J.
   May I kiss you? : a candid look at dating, communication, respect, & sexual
assault awareness/Michael J. Domitrz.—1st ed.
   Milwaukee, WI : Awareness Publications, 2003.
      p.   cm.
   ISBN 0-9729282-0-0
      1. Man-woman relationships. 2. Dating (Social customs)
   3. Interpersonal communication. 4. Communication and sex. 5. Rape Prevention.

HQ801 .D66 2003
306.73—dc21

Project Coordination by Printstar Publishing

Published by

**AWARENESS
PUBLICATIONS**

P.O. Box 20906 • Greenfield WI 53220-0906
800-329-9650 • www.awarenesspublications.com

*This book is available at quantity discounts.
For information, call 800-329-9650.*

Praise for *May I Kiss You?*

May I Kiss You? is not only a "must read" for students but for every adult as well. The realities of dating and intimacy are something that everyone needs to be aware of. It is important to have something that directs this issue at young men as well as young women.
Susan Kouns, Rape Victim Services
Pathways Inc., Ashland, Kentucky

Domitrz covers a sensitive topic in a unique manner. . . . He makes you think about the very basic "kiss" and how even that act demands permission.
Catherine Lovecchio, Director of Health & Wellness Education
Villanova University

A good, common sense approach to creating respectful relationships and avoiding assault, including guidelines for good communication, tips for preventing sexual assault, understanding its trauma, and helping a survivor. This book will be valuable for any young person who is thinking about what kind of relationships they want and how to ensure that they are healthy.
Alan Berkowitz, PhD, Independent Consultant
Trumansburg, New York

The book speaks to teens while informing parents and teachers. Domitrz speaks to both genders rather than focusing just on what girls need to do to not be victimized.
Jennifer Hegge, Educational Resources Coordinator
Wisconsin Coalition Against Sexual Assault

May I Kiss You? takes the discomfort out of talking about sexual intimacy and tells the facts in a straight-forward manner.
Julie A. Kruk, MS, LPC, Licensed Professional Counselor
Howard–Suamico School District, Bay Port High School, Wisconsin

Great information! Each section intrigues the reader to read on. Most important, Domitrz gives the reader exercises to help reinforce the concepts introduced throughout the book.
Sharlene Stewart, Parent of College Student
Immaculata, Pennsylvania

It's a subject that needs to be addressed, and this book does so with humor and a light, yet serious enough, tone. It presents a wealth of information for teens and adults alike.

Suzanne Trummer, ATODA Coordinator
Watertown Unified School District, Watertown, Wisconsin

Domitrz simplifies the confusion of the dating process by urging readers to openly communicate their wants and needs. He empowers both males and females to transcend stereotypical gender roles and embrace a relationship that is free from sexual pressure and misunderstandings.

Theresa Asmus, Counselor, Rape Crisis Service of Planned Parenthood
of the Rochester/Syracuse Region, New York

May I Kiss You? gives a healthy, straight-forward method for ensuring respectful dating behavior. Domitrz puts into words what we've known but haven't explained very well.

Patti Broomell, Counselor
Hamilton-Sussex High School, Sussex, Wisconsin

It is so wonderful to see sexual assault awareness being addressed by a male. The book challenges all of us to take a look at ourselves, our actions, and the ability that we all have to promote change!

Laura Pennimpede, Rape Crisis Community Educator
Victims Assistance Services

Domitrz's work is insightful, identifying the problems that can arise when men and women rely solely on body language, assumptions and interpretation to guide their actions.

Youth Today (September 2004)

May I Kiss You? provides valuable information to teenagers in simple, easy to understand terminology. It challenges them to think about their roles in relationships.

Paula Sonsalla, School Counselor
Pittsville Elementary (K-8), Pittsville, Wisconsin

May I Kiss You? has the very highest recommendation for all . . . and should be readily available in every high-school, college, and community library in the country.

Midwest Book Review (September 2003)

May I Kiss You?

With special thanks

Cheri Zimdars	Rita Hookstead
Joan Domitrz	Joe Domitrz
Marilyn Hamilton	Kay Lewis
Janet Simkus	Paul Simkus
Patty Hendrickson	Scott Thomas
Jerry Witherill	Ed Wegner
Sean Stephenson	Nick Laird
Larry Winget	Susan Pittelman
Peter Browne	Georgene Schreiner
Victor Gonzalez	Alan Berkowitz
Joseph Weinberg	Michael Karpovich

My wife, Karen, and our four boys
for their love and support.

To my incredible sister, Cheri

Thank you for your strength, courage, and love.
You have been the inspiration behind all of my work.
You continue to be a model for all survivors.

I love you, Cheri!

May I Kiss You?

CONTENTS

Introduction

Have you ever been on a date? Do you plan on dating? Are you single? Are you married with children? Do you know a student or an educator? Do you know other human beings? Pretty much covers the whole gamut of society, doesn't it? If you answered, "Yes" to any of these questions, this book is for you!

Educators want a book students can relate to, a book that inspires individuals to act with more respect toward one another, a book that serves as a continual resource for simple answers to tough questions.

Parents want a book to help them talk with their children about dating and intimacy.

Teenagers and young adults want honest and down-to-earth solutions they can use without feeling like idiots or "dorks."

From this demand, *May I Kiss You?* was written. Whether you have never dated or have been dating for years, this book will challenge you to evaluate the beliefs society has taught us about dating, communication, and respect.

While reading this book, you will relate to many situations. At the same time, you may find yourself saying, "I never looked at it that way before." Once you see the new perspective, you will want to make a change—a change you didn't expect.

The Inspiration

In the fall of 1989, my world abruptly halted when I received a devastating call from my mom. My sister had been raped. Over the next two years, everything I believed about dating was challenged. My own self worth was questioned. I went from wanting to kill my sister's rapist to looking at myself in the mirror and saying, "Who am I to judge?"

I asked my friends, "How do you date?" and soon learned that the average male's actions on a date were not far from the motivations of a serial rapist. Males were assuming what women wanted and then acting upon their own assumptions. Our society was teaching females to accept this unhealthy dating culture. A change was desperately needed.

After hearing a speaker on sexual assault address the school I was attending, a realization struck me. Each person can make a difference! I gathered all of the information I could on the subject of sexual assault. Then, I researched, researched, and did some more research. With all this knowledge, I created an interactive program on dating, communication, and respect to help reduce the occurrence of sexual assault.

Educators and students told me people needed to hear my challenging and life-changing message. Today, I travel the country sharing the lessons in this book with people of all ages!

What's Inside

May I Kiss You? is about more than sexual assault. You will find the pages filled with challenging questions, thought-provoking scenarios, dynamic solutions, and life-changing philosophies. While you can find books detailing research and statistics, *May I Kiss You?* provides a unique perspective.

May I Kiss You? is an in-depth look at dating, communication, respect, and the importance of sexual assault awareness. If you understand the concepts in this book and then live your life accordingly, you will have a lot more fun dating. You will experience healthier intimacy in your current and future relationships.

The added benefit? You will date with a greater awareness for yourself and your dating partner. By doing so, you will help reduce the number of uncomfortable dating situations. You will help reduce the number of sexual assaults occurring in the world.

Are you ready? You are about to take a journey that will cause you to laugh, to think quietly, and to look in the mirror. Let the reading begin!

Are You Average?

What does "average" mean? Do you respond in dating situations the same way most people would respond? As you read this book, decide when and how you fit the following statements:

◆ In some situations, I follow the norms of dating.
◆ In some situations, I defy the norms of dating.

Each person can provide a different answer for every question in this book. To keep the book concise, fun to read, and powerful, we will be taking a close look at the "average" response given by a person.

When your answer is different from the average, do not be disappointed. Unique results can be positive. Simply recognize why your answer was different and then ask yourself, "Is this good, or should I make a change?" As you read the book, you will learn how to tell the difference.

On the average date, how does the way I respect my partner and communicate with my partner relate to sexual assault? In spending time with people from around the world, I have never met anyone who believed he/she intentionally assaulted a dating partner. People do not notice their own behaviors until they are given a new perspective. Once people's eyes are opened to the realities of dating, they share their stories of confusion, disrespect, and assault.

No one is immune to this important societal problem. I believed "I was not the type, nor were my friends" and "I could never sexually assault someone"—until the day my mom called to tell me that my sister had been raped. That call changed my life and inspired me to make changes.

No professional or expert can guarantee 100% prevention of sexual assault or unhealthy dating situations. However, the more prepared you are with knowledge and awareness, the more you decrease your odds of experiencing or contributing to this horrific trauma.

May I Kiss You? is full of direct and upfront conversation concerning dating, communication, respect, and sexual assault awareness. The questions and issues you will be challenged with exist in all types of dating and intimate relationships (including all sexual orientations and all levels of intimacy). While the book mainly focuses on young heterosexual couples, you can transfer the lessons and stories to all couples. *So—Are you ready for a challenge?*

ONE

The LOOK
You Know What I Mean

Have you ever felt nervous about dating? Do you wonder what your date is going to think of you? Do you worry about how the date is going to end? To understand dating, the dangers involved, and how to build wonderful relationships, we must first comprehend the way we communicate on dates.

Body language is the most common form of communication in dating. For example, do most people ask before they kiss someone? No. Instead, they try to figure out when is the right time to make their "move." How do they figure out when is the right time? By reading body language.

The world of dating relies heavily on sending and receiving body language signals. Is body language reliable? No. If it were, you would know when someone wanted to be intimate with you. You would never experience confusing moments in the beginning of intimacy or during intimacy. You would always know how comfortable your partner was with you. Occurrences of sexual assaults could be greatly reduced.

Are you good at reading body language? Are you great at sending the right "messages" to your dates? Take this Body Language Challenge. If you have a group of people, each of you take the test individually and then share your answers.

TAKING THE BODY LANGUAGE CHALLENGE

Challenge No. 1:

Imagine you are single; an attractive person is sitting across the room from you. Send the person messages through your body language to tell him/her you want to go on a date. Will the person interpret your signals perfectly? For a fun exercise, try this with another person. Remember, this person has to interpret your body language correctly.

Challenge No. 2:

Write down all of the body language signals used by individuals on a date to communicate with each other. Include every signal imaginable. Example: moving closer to someone to let the person know you like him/her.

Challege No. 3:

A man and woman are walking down the beach together on a date. As they hold hands, the man can feel the woman's hands are sweaty and tightly holding onto his. Write down how the man is likely to read her signals. Next, write down what feelings the woman might be experiencing to cause her tight grip and sweaty palms.

Challenge No. 4:

During a date, the woman is having a great time and really likes the guy. The two of them are sitting closely together. To let him know she likes him, she places her hand on his knee. Write how you think he will read this signal from the woman. Be detailed in your answer.

Challenge No. 5:

Have you ever heard someone say, "When he gave me 'the look,' I just knew what he wanted?" People often refer to the "look" when describing romantic moments. How would you describe your version of the "look"? Write a detailed description of the look you would give another person to let him/her know you are interested. Ask a friend to try this challenge and then share your answers with each other.

Challenge No. 6:

Write the amount of time two people can exhaust trying to read each other's body language before one tries to kiss the other. Example: a male and female are alone and sitting together in a private place. Both of them want to kiss each other, but are not verbally asking. They are making conversation while trying to read each other's body language. How long could pass before one of them actually tries to kiss the other?

Have you completed all six steps of the Body Language Challenge? Each of the challenges are real situations that can occur every day of the week. Let's see how well you did.

DISCUSSING THE BODY LANGUAGE CHALLENGE

Challenge No. 1:

If you tried this challenge with another person, did either of you laugh? The reason people will start laughing during this exercise is because each of you realizes how silly you look trying to send body language signals. While trying to read another person's body language, you feel like you are trying to read their mind. Reading minds is a skill most people admit they don't posssess. If you can't read minds, body language does not work.

For body language to be an effective means of communication, everyone needs to use the same "signals." Since every person reads "signals" differently, you cannot guarantee the correct interpretation of body language.

Challenge No. 2:

Are you done writing all the body language signals? For fun, share the answers with other people. If you wrote down every possible body language signal, you would be writing for days (flirting for fun, letting a person know you want him/her, sending the signal you want to kiss, etc.). Since an infinite number of "signals" exist, knowing all of them is impossible.

Challenge No. 3:

Male's Reaction: "If she is holding my hand tightly, she likes me. She is letting me know she enjoys holding my hand. She might even have strong feelings for me. The sweaty palms are telling me she is nervous and she wants everything to go right . . . another sign she really likes me."

4

Female's Reaction: "My hands are sweaty because I am nervous. He has made some comments during the date that make me feel uncomfortable. In fact, I am a little scared being alone with him as we walk down the beach. I want to pull my hand away from his, but I don't know how he will react. I don't want to get him mad, especially with us being all alone out here. I was holding his hand tightly? I didn't even notice. Must have been my nerves."

The male and female were experiencing the exact same body language, yet each had completely different reactions to her signals. These misunderstandings can happen on any date.

How about this?

Write down situations in which a person could misread a date's body language. Be specific on how the person could misread the body language. In many cases, you could have multiple possibilities for reading the same body language.

Example

In Challenge No. 3, what else could the woman have been trying to tell her date? How else could the man have read her body language?

Challenge No. 4:

Will he think, "Oh, how nice. She is putting her hand on my knee to let me know she is interested in me"? More likely, he will say to himself, "Yes! She wants me!" When a male thinks, "She wants me," he may start to believe she wants to be highly sexually involved with him (more than kissing).

5

Is there a difference between "liking" a guy and "wanting" him? The difference can be gigantic and can lead to tremendous assumptions and problems. Challenge No. 4 shows how one commonly used body language signal can lead to confusion and misunderstanding.

Challenge No. 5:

Did you find it hard to describe your "look"? If you shared the description of your "look" with a friend, was either of you laughing? The reality is that one standard "look" does not exist. Every person has a completely different "look." To understand another person's "look," everyone would have to know each other's distinct expressions, and each expression could only have one meaning.

If body language worked, you would know precisely what the person was thinking when he/she gave you a "look." On a date, a female would know if the male wanted to kiss her. She could send him a look to tell him the way she liked being kissed. He would know precisely how far she wanted to go. All of this information just from a "look"? Is that possible? No.

Picture a man named Kevin walking into a party where tons of people are crammed in the room. After being at the party for a while, he scopes out the crowd. He notices one gorgeous woman. She is everything he wants in a woman. As his eyes are stuck gazing upon her, she turns. She looks over his way. This moment is the very opportunity he has been waiting for. He gives a nod toward her as he smiles with a look of "Hey, how are you doing?" smacked across his face. A smile comes across her face—as if she had been waiting to see him.

6

Kevin feels incredible. He turns to his friends in a voice filled with nervous energy and says, "Did you see her looking at me? I think she was checking me out. Did you see how she smiled at me?" The group of guys start smirking and John, a friend, says, "Do you mean the girl over there?" "Yes, her," says Kevin. John replies, "The same girl waving and smiling to the guy right behind you?" Kevin turns. He realizes the woman was not looking at him. She was looking at another guy who was standing behind him.

Does the above scenario happen? Yes, every day of the week to thousands of people. Embarrassing? Most definitely and most of us have experienced this type of humiliation (at school, a concert, a party, etc.).

Why do we think the person is looking at us? Because being recognized in a positive manner feels good. Being wanted creates an even more powerful rush. When we interpret body language, we often project our hopes and wants onto the other person. By doing so, we see what we WANT to see.

How about this?

Have you ever enjoyed helping another person but then the person thought you were attracted to him/her? Why did the person think you were attracted to him/her? Many times people assume someone being nice to another person is a sign of attraction.

Write down specific examples of how this can happen at work or school or with a group of friends. How do you react when the person misunderstands your "being nice"? What is the most respectful way you could react in these situations?

> **Example**
>
> *A guy is helping one of his classmates with her homework. As they are working on homework, they are laughing and having a great time together. The woman goes home and tells her sister that she thinks the guy is interested in her.*

When the woman at the party looked toward Kevin, he wanted her to desire him and so he believed that she did. When you are on a date, you want to believe that the other person finds you attractive. You look for signs confirming the attraction. Here is the problem. You are LOOKING for signs showing the person is attracted to you. By doing so, your mind can interpret any sign as a positive sign, a sign of attraction. Everyone subconsciously participates in this progression of thoughts.

This projection of thoughts and wants can be extremely harmful in dating situations and relationships. Once you think the other person wants something, you might go after it. You make an intimate move on your partner (a form of sexual contact) because you assume this person wants it. However, he/she didn't want it. Now, you have sexually assaulted your date! This danger is why relying on body language is a horrible way to communicate.

Challenge No. 6:

How much time did you think would pass before a kiss was attempted? From five minutes to over two hours is the common answer to this challenge. A college student once told me, "I waited the entire date. I just kept waiting for him to kiss me and he never did."

If body language worked, you would only take seconds to know the "right time" to kiss. Why don't we know in just seconds? Because reading another person's body language is problematic. In fact, it is a GUESS. Whether you wait five minutes or two hours to read someone's signals before you make your move to kiss, will you then know for certain the other person wants to kiss? No, you will not. *Unless you directly ask, you are always taking a guess.* Asking is the only way you can positively know if the other person does or does not want to be intimate with you.

The Body Language Challenge showed you multiple examples of how body language can cause confusion and misunderstanding between two people on a date or in a relationship. Each of the examples is a real-life scenario that frequently happens to people. Each challenge proved body language is not effective. We need to use a better form of communication.

CHAPTER ONE: THE LOOK

Remember this

- ◆ Body language is unreliable!
- ◆ Relying on body language is dangerous.
- ◆ While on a date, do not project or force your wants onto the other person.

Try this

Watch people in a public place. Notice the body language each person sends as he or she passes by other people. Now try to notice when people talk to each other. Write down the way people interact when talking is involved. Describe their expressions and animation. See if you notice how people's expressions and emotions come alive as they talk.

9

Bonus *(Chapter 1)*

 Strictly Students: Discover 2 tips to correctly using body language at www.mayikissyou.com/students.

 Parents Pointers: Find out what messages you are sending to your child at www.mayikissyou.com/parents.

 Teachers Tool: Get 3 extra questions to discuss with your students at www.mayikissyou.com/educators.

TWO

Talking?
You Must Be Kidding

Walk up to a person and say, "Before you kiss someone on a date, do you ask for permission?" How do you think the person is going to respond? First, you may hear the person laugh. You might notice the person looking at you with a "you must be kidding" look on his/her face. Finally, the person will probably respond with "No way would I ask."

Why doesn't everyone ask? FEAR! Fear can be a strong factor in the choices people make. The Dating Fear Factors below are the three reasons why people do not ask for permission before kissing or becoming intimate with another person.

- ◆ Rejection
- ◆ Image destruction
- ◆ Humiliation

Fear of Rejection

When you avoid asking for a kiss, you are anticipating that a verbal rejection will be more humiliating than a rejection from

11

just "making your move." You fear hearing the word "No" would be devastating to your confidence. Could that possibly be worse than the alternative—perhaps not to you—but what about your date's feelings?

"Not asking" can result in embarrassing and dangerous consequences. If you don't ask and just try your "moves" on someone, the person could push you away, slap you, turn away from you, or worse. All of these "nonverbal" reactions are forms of rejection.

If you just try without asking, what do you do when the other person doesn't react? If you kiss someone and he/she does not respond in a negative manner, you might assume the person wants you to continue. However, the person may be too uncomfortable to speak out. The person may be worried about creating a difficult situation by negatively reacting to you. In the meantime, you think everything is going great. In reality, you are creating very uncomfortable circumstances.

As you read this, did you think to yourself, "I could tell if someone did not want me to kiss him/her"? Have you ever known one person to return from a date talking about how awesome the date went? The person told you what a great "end of date" kiss they experienced. At the same time, the other person on the date is telling people how boring the date was and how awful the kiss at the end went. We all know this happens.

You don't ask because you fear being rejected. You just try to make your "move." Now you are rejected by being pushed away or slapped. Where is the date headed at this point? The date is probably over and you have ruined any chance to get to know this

12

person. Why? Because you were afraid to ask. Your fear drove you to act with disrespect for the other person's feelings. Believing in your fear caused you to make another person uncomfortable. The worst result of not asking is committing a sexual assault. Asking for consent eliminates the danger and the embarrassment.

Fear of Image Destruction

You fear your image will be destroyed when everyone hears that you asked for a kiss. Males fear looking less like a "man" or not appearing "macho." Males fear peers calling them a "wimp." Females fear getting a reputation for being sexually aggressive. Females fear being called "easy" and other sexually derogatory names. Men and women fear their sexuality being questioned.

How do you get past the fear of your image being ruined? If you think the person you are dating will degrade you for asking, do not go on the date! Any time you fear what your dating partner is going to say about you, you are entering into an unhealthy and potentially hazardous dating environment.

Honor the highest standards for yourself. When going on a date, expect to be respected. Only date people who respect you. The moment you feel a lack of respect, recognize the danger and do everything you can to get out of the situation.

Fear of Humiliation

You fear looking like an idiot or a fool in front of your date. This is the number one reason people do not verbally ask for permission to kiss or to be intimate. You fear asking will make you look bad or will take away the romance of the moment.

The reason you have this negative view of asking is because

you never see or hear role models ask. Consider your favorite television shows and movies. How often do you see the characters ask before they kiss? How about adults in your life? If you cannot find positive examples on television or the movies, do not worry. Characters live in a "fake" world where no one gets sexually assaulted. You live in the real world. Set the standard and be the positive example for others. *Ask!*

How about this?

Describe the "average" scene of intimacy you watch on television or in a movie. How do the two people approach each other? How do television and the movies try to make intimacy look easy and "perfect"? Think of all the differences in a "real" date verses a movie or television date. Write down all of the flaws in the "average" television or movie scene of romance.

Example

On television, the man walks into his house. He sees his partner across the room. Music starts playing. He goes toward her and just starts romantically kissing her. They never say anything to each other. What would happen if the average guy tried this? What would his partner think?

Dating Gender Gap

The concern over being humiliated is resolved by talking to the other gender. One of the biggest problems with learning how to date is that you are likely to learn only from your own gender. Males learn from males. Females learn from females. When this happens, you tend to hear about stereotypes such as:

Males saying, *"Women only want the 'bad' guy."*
Females saying, *"All guys are out for only one thing."*

These stereotypes produce a negative image of the other gender. This image results in males and females assuming things about each other, instead of talking to each other. Thus, the creation of the Dating Gender Gap!

Male Dating Gender Gap

Males believe asking a female for a kiss is "wimpy" and would ruin the moment. The reality is that women find asking to be very romantic. A man asking is unique. Asking makes him stand out from the rest of the guys. Asking shows he cares and only wants to do something with the woman if she wants to. Lastly, asking helps eliminate the female's image of "men wanting only one thing."

Female Dating Gender Gap

There are two primary reasons females do not take the initiative to ask men for a kiss. One reason is the belief that "asking is the man's job." The other reason is women believe a man would be turned off by a woman asking for a kiss.

Actually, many men find assertive women attractive. Guys do not like having all the pressure of "knowing when to make the moves." When a woman asks a guy for a kiss, he knows she wants the kiss. All of the pressure is off him. Men often feel stressed about making this decision. With Challenge No. 6 in Chapter One, we showed how many hours a person may wait before making this decision. Why? The person fears being wrong about reading the other's body language.

Believing it is the "man's job" to ask leads to an unbalanced relationship. The healthiest relationships are when two people have equal respect for each other. Once you believe the other person has more control over the decision to be intimate, you are not equal. You are surrendering a degree of power.

Never give up your self-respect! For males and females to have equality, we must live by the standard of equality in every facet of our relationships. Most men do not want the "job" of being the aggressor. If a woman wants something, the man wants the woman to tell him. Have you ever heard a man say, "She expects me to read her mind. I wish she would just tell me"?

If a woman feels a certain way or wants something, she should say it. Empower women to speak their minds freely. For centuries, our culture worked against the concept of equality. Each of us needs to do our best to continue creating equality and equal respect for everyone.

The key to eliminating the Dating Gender Gap is talking with the other gender. Ask specific questions about how the other gender feels.

How about this?

Write down questions you would like to ask the other gender. Talk to your friends and find out what questions they would like to ask the other gender. Get a group of males and females together and discuss the questions. Have each gender answer all the questions. Do not ridicule anyone for his/her question. Talk to each other with respect and understanding.

Talk with people who have experienced asking or being asked for a kiss. You might have to talk to a lot of people before you find someone with experience being asked. Keep trying until you find someone. Get their honest opinion of what it felt like. You will learn how much people appreciate and enjoy being asked.

If you want to learn how to make lots of money, do you ask a person who constantly loses money? No, you ask the person who has success making lots of money. Do the same with dating. Ask the person who has experience in showing respect for their partners by asking.

CHAPTER TWO: TALKING?

Remember this

- I have no reasons for not asking!
- Talk to people who have experienced asking.

Try this

Get a group of friends together to play the Dating Gender Gap game. Have the women write down all of the stereotypes they can think of about men. Have the men write down all of the stereotypes they can think of about women. Put each stereotype on a separate piece of paper. Separate the stereotypes into two piles (male and female). Each team has to randomly pick a piece of paper with a stereotype from the pile and then explain why their gender is known for that stereotype. The other team can counter that gender with ways the stereotype could be eliminated. This game can be very silly, lots of fun, and really get everyone thinking.

Example

The men pick up a piece of paper that the women wrote about the men. The paper says, "Men try to be macho on dates." The men explain why they do this and then the women tell the men why they hate men doing that. You can have lots of people laughing and learning! Now the challenge is for the women to give examples of what they like.

Bonus

 Strictly Students: Find how you may be discriminating at www.mayikissyou.com/students.

 Parents Pointers: Get the secret to creating equality for your son or daughter in relationships at www.mayikissyou.com/parents.

 Teachers Tool: Discover how to encourage males and females speaking out at www.mayikissyou.com/educators.

THREE

The Time Is Now
Do You Know How?

At this point, you know that body language is not reliable. You have eliminated all reasons for not asking. You have no excuses for not showing the highest level of respect for your dating partner by asking before you try kissing.

So what is the last hurdle? Inexperience. Trying something you have never seen done is difficult. At first, asking may seem challenging, but remember, as long as you ask in a respectful manner, there is no "wrong" way to ask for a kiss.

The key to asking is keeping one thought in the forefront of your mind: why you are asking. You are asking because you do not want to make the other person feel uncomfortable. You are asking because you do not want to do something to another person you will regret. Once you touch someone, you can't act like it didn't happen. You are asking because you care and respect the person you are with. For these reasons, you will ask with a caring and respectful approach.

Is asking romantic? This is a common question people have. Being romantic is treating your date with compassion, respect, and care. Asking is the ultimate sign of romance. Both males and females are attracted to people who ask. Examine the two scenarios below. As you read the "Female Asks" and the "Male Asks" sections, choose whether you think most people would respond with Option No. 1 or Option No. 2.

FEMALE ASKS

Two people, Kevin and Michelle, are alone at the end of a date. The night is going really well. Michelle turns to Kevin and says, "I have a question I really want to ask you." Kevin says, "What is the question?" Michelle asks, "May I kiss you?" Assuming Kevin wanted to be kissed, how do you think he will react to being asked?

Option No. 1

Kevin says, "I can't believe you just asked. You are a woman. You are not supposed to ask. Now you ruined it for me."

Option No. 2

A smile quickly comes across Kevin's face as he says, "Yes!"

MALE ASKS

Kevin and Michelle are alone at the end of a date. The night is going really well. Kevin turns to Michelle and says "I have a question I really want to ask you." Michelle says, "What is the question?" Kevin stumbles over his words as he asks, "May I kiss you?" Assuming Michelle wants to be kissed, how will she react to being asked?

Option No. 1

Michelle says, "What are you doing asking? If you ask, something is wrong with you."

Option No. 2

Michelle smiles in pleasant surprise as she answers, "Yes!"

Which option did you pick in the "Male Asks" and "Female Asks" scenes? Most people will pick Option No. 2 for both scenes.

Assuming both people want to kiss, how could anyone truly be "turned off" by being asked? The examples above show how foolish the concept "asking is not romantic" sounds. If a friend tells you, "Asking will ruin the moment," present both options from above. Help your friend realize how this statement lacks common sense.

How about this?

What if you did ask someone and the person answered with the responses from Option No. 1? What would you do? This is the perfect time to open up conversation between the two of you. Learn why the person has these beliefs of male and female "roles" with intimacy. The person may have low self-esteem and not understand the need for someone to show respect toward a date.

Discuss this person's views of dating. Be supportive. Write down every answer you think of. Discuss your answers with friends to decide which approach is both reasonable and respectful.

Ask yourself, "When I ask for a kiss, which person would I prefer to ask?" The person who responded with Option No. 1 or the person who responded with Option No. 2? Hopefully, you are going to pick the person in Option No. 2. Why? The person appears to be considerate, appreciative, and respectful.

Did you catch a potential problem with the previous two examples? The earlier dialogues discuss two people who want to kiss each other. Does this always happen? No. How do you handle being turned down?

Rejection – You Choose!

Do you remember how you can be rejected if you don't ask and you just "make a move"? Getting slapped, hit, pushed away, or given the cold shoulder are just a few forms of the physical rejection you can experience. Once you are physically rejected by someone, in what direction is the date going? In a downward spiral!

When you ask for a kiss, what is the most likely form of getting turned down? Hearing the word "No" and then hearing a reason. The reasons could vary from "I don't kiss on the first date" to "I don't think now is the right time" or "I am not comfortable enough with our relationship."

Reacting to being turned down is the tough part. You asked because you wanted to show total respect for the other person. Now, he or she has turned you down. What do you say? What do you do? Is this date doomed?

Let the person know why you asked. In a caring and relieved voice, say, "Then I am glad I asked, because the last thing I would want to do is make you feel uncomfortable." Across the country, females react to this sentence with a heartfelt "Awww" and the guys react by saying "Smooth." Both genders have an amazingly positive reaction. Why?

> *Are you using a "line" on the person? No. A "line" is a made-up or contrived comment to try and impress the other person. Most "lines" fail miserably. Why is this comment not a line? Because telling someone, "Then I am glad I asked, because the last thing I would want to do is make you feel uncomfortable" is the real reason you are asking. You ARE asking because you don't want to make the other person uncomfortable. By making this statement, all you are doing is telling the TRUTH!*

After sharing the truth, where is the date going? Is the date ruined or spiraling downward? No. Can you still make this date a success? Yes. In fact, the relationship between the two of you may be stronger after this experience. You have created a level of equal respect between the two of you. When presented with this option, possible responses from each gender are listed below:

Female who said "No" to a kiss, responds by saying,

"I never expected him to ask, especially the way he handled my saying 'No.' By his accepting my not wanting to kiss him, he showed me he is not just on this date to 'get something' from me. He actually appears to sincerely care about me. This makes me want to get to know him better."

Male who said "No" to a kiss, responds by saying,

"Wow! The way the date was going, I just felt no connection between the two of us and didn't feel like kissing her. When she asked me for a kiss, I was really worried about how she

would take my saying 'No.' She was so cool about it. I found it easy for us to talk the rest of the date."

Being honest and open with each other can lead to more meaningful discussions. Imagine if everyone were honest on dates. You could learn if the two of you were dating each other for the same reasons. You could learn if the person had different intentions than you. You could stop a bad or dangerous date before it ever began.

How about this?

Write down several "wrong" reasons for someone to date you. Each person can have very different answers to this question. Next, write the reasons you want a person to date you.

Example

I don't want to date someone who is focused on how much money I have. I want someone to date me because they enjoy my sense of humor.

Two of the common concerns with asking for intimacy are below:

Asking for Intimacy Concern No. 1

"It is only a kiss. What is the big deal if you kiss someone and they don't want it?"

The kiss is the beginning of intimacy. The standard you establish in the beginning sets the tone for the rest of the relationship. Always set a high standard of respect right from the start.

24

Asking for Intimacy Concern No. 2

"Talking about 'doing something' with someone is too difficult. Just trying it with each other is much easier."

Doesn't the above comment lack common sense? If you are not comfortable talking about an act of intimacy with your partner, why are you engaging in the intimacy? When you realize you cannot talk to someone about a certain level of intimacy, you are not ready to engage in that level of intimacy. The golden rule of dating is: *If you can't talk about it, don't do it!*

How about this?

Get a group of males and females together. Role play the scene of a male asking a female for a kiss or an intimate act. First, have the man ask by trying to use a typical "line" with the female. Next, have the male ask in a concerned and straightforward fashion. Have the female answer "No" in one example and "Yes" in the other example.

The role play is a role play. Neither person should ever touch the other person or actually try to kiss the other person.

Now, reverse roles! Have the female ask both ways. Have the male answer "No" once and "Yes" the second time. How can you change the scenario one more time and try it again? After each attempt at asking, talk with everyone about what it looked like, sounded like, and felt like. When trying something for the first time, the best approach is practice, practice, and practice. By role playing with friends, you can practice without the threat of facing real rejection or embarrassment.

What about more than a kiss?

"Okay, I will definitely ask before I kiss someone, but what about more than a kiss? How do I ask someone if I can do specific intimate acts with them? Won't I take away the excitement?"

Being able to talk about intimacy is a sign of maturity and responsibility. By talking, each of you learns what acts of intimacy the other person enjoys doing the most. With this knowledge, you are more equipped to please each other.

Michelle, Kevin's wife, comes home and says, "Kevin, tonight I am going to put the kids to bed by 8:00 p.m. and then I want you to meet me in bed for some fun." Which of the following two responses is Kevin more likely to give? "I don't like it when we plan our intimacy or talk about it. No thanks."
OR
"Yes. I can't wait till 8:00 p.m."

As silly as this example may sound, everyone agrees Kevin is much more likely to be excited about 8:00 p.m. When you talk, the intimacy is more exciting because you look forward to experiencing the intimate acts you both enjoy the most. Regardless of being married or single, talking greatly improves intimacy.

Caution: Being intimate with a person can involve tremendous risks. No form of "100% safe sex" exists. If you decide to be intimately involved with another person, seek professional guidance on how to protect yourself from sexually transmitted disease and unintended pregnancy. Please be as safe as possible in your decisions.

Ask yourself, "Why am I choosing to engage in this activity with this person?" If the answer is "for fun" or "because I really like this person," remind yourself of all the risks and their potential impact on both your futures. If your partner has respect for you, he/she will honor your decision to wait. Respect yourself at all times.

Values List

Holding yourself to high standards is easier when you believe in yourself and your values. On a scale of 1 to 10, write down what you would score yourself as a person. Ten is the highest score and one is the lowest score. Ten is not perfect. Being a "10" simply means you believe you are the best person you can be.

You can be a "10." Did you score yourself a "10"? If you didn't score yourself a "10," do it now. Write a list of what makes you a "10." Write down every aspect of who you are that makes you unique, special, and valuable. Then, write a list with all of your personal values.

Get together with friends and review each person's list. While listening to your friends' lists, you will think of values you forgot about but that you know you believe in. Add those values to your list. After each person reads his or her list, encourage the group to tell him or her more items that can be added. Often friends see strengths and values in you that you don't notice. Now you have a large list of values. Cherish this list. When you wake up each morning, read it out loud (no one else has to hear you). Reading the list out loud will help tell your brain to honor these values and reinforce your image of self respect.

Examples of personal values can include:
"I do the right thing."
"I have compassion for others."
"I respect all people."
"My body is precious."

At the end of each day, ask yourself, "Did the actions and decisions I made today fit the values I believe in? Did today's actions and decisions add to my value?"

How about this?

Recall a time when you took an action or made a decision against your values, then decide why you made the negative choice. Write down the reason and how it resulted in a negative outcome. Did it make you feel bad? Did it make someone else feel bad? Would you do the same today? By noticing mistakes, you have the ability to steer away from a future negative choice.

Now recall a decision that added to your value; write it down. Write down why you made the choice and how that choice made you feel. Remind yourself how rewarding making a positive decision feels.

Once a week, get together with your friends and share your experiences. From school to dating, help each other stay away from bad choices. Applaud each other for making good choices. By sharing your decisions, your friends can help hold you accountable to your commitment of living with high standards and values.

What does creating a Values List have to do with healthy dating? When you possess positive values, people will be less likely to negatively affect your decision-making process. When you have values based on respect, you will not take actions to hurt another person. When you believe in your values, a date will be less likely to succeed in persuading you to partake in actions you are not comfortable with. You will speak more freely about your opinions and beliefs. You will reflect an image of strength and respect.

The healthiest relationships are built on respect. Respect for yourself and your partner. Respect through open and honest communication. Exercise respect for you and your partner by talking with each other. Remember the golden rule of intimacy: *If you can't talk about it, don't do it.*

CHAPTER THREE: THE TIME IS NOW

Remember this

- ◆ Ask with RESPECT.
- ◆ Asking is the ultimate sign of romance!
- ◆ Tell the person why you asked.
- ◆ Create open & honest conversations.
- ◆ Believe in your values. Add to your values.
- ◆ If you can't talk about it, don't try it!

Try this

Write a script of two people on a date. Create fun and respectful dialogue that reinforces the strength in talking and asking. Donate the script to a local school for its health classes to use as a role-playing scene between students.

Bonus *(Chapter 3)*

 Strictly Students: Read the biggest fear many people have for not asking at www.mayikissyou.com/students.

 Parents Pointers: Take the *"Respect Survey"* for your family at www.mayikissyou.com/parents.

 Teachers Tool: Get the *"What If"* exercise at www.mayikissyou.com/educators.

FOUR

Do I Have to Ask?
Why?

Could you sexually assault another person? While most people answer "No," many of these same people have already committed a sexual assault. Did you know a sexual assault occurs on the average date when a couple becomes sexually intimate for the first time? How can this be?

To understand, you have to know the meaning of sexual assault. While the legal definition of sexual assault may vary by state, in this book sexual assault is defined as:

sexual contact without consent.

Like other crimes, states can have varying degrees of sexual assault (first degree, second degree, third degree, and fourth degree). The lowest degree may be sexual contact without consent. Sexual intercourse without consent would be a higher degree of sexual assault.

Briefly write down what the word "consent" means to you. If you want consent to borrow something from another person, what do you do? You need to ask.

Do people ask before they kiss or touch someone in an intimate area? Not usually! We know people assume consent by trying to read body language—body language that we have learned is unreliable. Since most people do not receive consent, they are acting under the parameters of a sexual assault. Thus, a sexual assault is likely to happen on a date where a couple is becoming intimate for the first time.

To help discover the need for changes in the way we approach intimacy, read the following paragraph. Ask yourself if this example could be a typical date. Ask yourself if you know people who have been on this type of a date.

Two of your friends are going on a date together for the first time. Both are nice people who you enjoy being friends with. The male friend asked your female friend out because he is attracted to her. As the date advances, he feels comfortable with her. He thinks she wants to be intimate with him. At this point, he tries to kiss her. He thinks she wants the kiss, and so he continues. Over time, he touches her more intimately. He continues advancing the touching until she stops him. He stops.

Where is the sexual assault? Think about when he stopped. He only stopped when she took action to stop him. How uncomfortable would most women be before they took physical or strong verbal action to stop a man? Across the country, I ask audiences of women this very question. The average woman says she will not normally take action to stop a man unless she is very uncomfortable with his actions or he is already doing something she did not want him to do. By the point she is trying to stop him, he has gone too far. A sexual assault has already taken place.

Sexual assailants try to argue that the woman gave "implied" consent because she did not do anything to stop him earlier in the date. If you don't say anything or take any action, are you giving consent? No! As we have learned, gaining consent means getting someone's permission. Permission requires a response. If I do not respond, I have not given permission.

Try using "implied" consent as an excuse for robbery. You are walking down the street and I approach you. As I get near you, I pull a gun out and tell you to give me all your money. You freeze. You don't say anything. I take your money and run off. However, I get caught and go to trial for robbery.

In this robbery case, my defense attorney is going to argue you gave "implied consent" for me to take your money. How? You didn't tell me "not to take your money" or to stop robbing you. You must have wanted me to take your money. Does this defense of "implied consent" sound ridiculous? Yes. Sadly, some sexual assault assailants have successfully used a similar defense of "implied consent" against their victims.

Is comparing sexual assault to robbery a bad example? Yes, because being sexually assaulted is much more traumatic than being robbed. The comparison is clearly not fair to victims of sexual assault.

Why didn't your female friend on the date speak up or stop him sooner? This question is repeatedly asked by society. What is the inherent problem with this question? The question implies

33

it was the woman's responsibility to stop the man's actions. Did she take the action or did he?

From the scenario you read, the man took the action. When you choose to assert yourself upon another person, who is responsible for your actions? You are! Therefore, the man in this example was responsible. You cannot blame the woman for the man's choices.

When did he get consent? He didn't. He never knew that she definitely wanted any of the intimate actions he took. He couldn't know because he didn't ask. Imagine proving that you had consent when you did not ask. You can never blame the victim for the assailant's actions.

Was the friend in the previous story a horrible person? No, this is a man you consider to be a good friend. Sexual assault is rarely about "bad guys" or scary strangers. Sexual assault is more routinely about the average couple. Sexual assault can happen when two good people are dating each other and one person acts with disregard for the other person's feelings and rights.

More frequently, the man is the aggressor. Does the aggressor always intentionally hurt the victim? Not necessarily, but that factor doesn't matter. If you hurt someone, your ignorance or your intentions do not erase or decrease the victim's pain and trauma. To avoid this kind of escalation, it is necessary to turn your thoughts into words.

Who do you center your thoughts on? If you think, "Do I have to ask?" you are thinking of yourself first. "Do I have to?" sounds like someone having to clean their room or mow the lawn. You appear to be annoyed by having to ask. In the case of dating, you are talking about the respect of another person's mind and body—not a minor issue of annoyance.

When you think "I need to ask," you are placing your dating partner as an equal to yourself. Comprehending and believing in the need to ask is essential. Out of respect for the person, you need to ask. The best thought process is, "I want to ask." "I want to ask" is a positive statement and will leave a stronger impression in your mind.

Respect & the Law

What is your mental focus on a date? Focusing strictly on the law is not the best way to approach a date. When individuals consider the law, many regularly think, "I won't get caught" or "How can I get around the law?" Should you learn the law in your state? Yes. Once you know and understand the law, focus on respect. If you act with the utmost respect for your dating partner and for yourself, you will not need to concentrate only on the law. Consider the harm to others, not just the risk to yourself.

On a date, disregard for the law is likely to result in disrespecting your partner. If you think, "How can I get around asking to be intimate?" you are taking the risk of hurting the other person. Hurting another person or making a person uncomfortable is not a risk to take on a date. *Dating with respect is much more fun and is safer for everyone.*

Wanting to act respectfully will inspire you to ask before becoming more intimately involved. Respect is the key to safe and healthy dating.

Long-term Relationships

After you have asked a person for the first kiss, do you need to continue to ask for further intimacy? Yes. Each person can have a different comfort level with intimacy. To learn each other's boundaries, talk to each other. The process of talking to each other helps create a comfort level between both people and a stronger foundation for future intimacy.

If you are married, do you still need consent? Yes. Husbands and wives can, and have, sexually assaulted their partners. Whether you have been dating for three months or have been married for forty years, no person owes sexual or intimate acts to their partner. It is NOT a boyfriend's, a girlfriend's, a wife's, or a husband's job to be sexually active with his/her partner. People in long-term relationships and marriages still need consent. Talk with each other to ensure that each person wants the intimacy. Regardless of how long the relationship has existed, mutual respect is essential in all relationships.

How about this?

What are challenges that couples in long-term relationships face with communicating, talking, and getting consent? Analyze each of your answers and find a solution that emphasizes respect. Try role playing each challenge and solution.

Example

Once they have been intimate together, one of the people assumes intimacy is his/her right whenever he/she wants it. You could explain that each act of intimacy is separate from the last act. In all cases, both people need to "want" the intimacy.

While most examples in this chapter have been males sexually assaulting females, sexual assault can be committed by anyone of any age, male or female. There is no standard "image" of a sexual assault assailant, except the one you place inside your mind.

Could you sexually assault another person? What actions will you take to ensure you never commit a sexual assault? Write down what you are going to do differently to ensure that you will never commit a sexual assault. When you complete the list, read your answers out loud. Why write down your answers and then read the answers out loud? The brain more effectively retains information presented to it in various formats—reading, writing, and speaking.

Once you feel comfortable with making your statements out loud, share your ideas with other people. Your actions to stop sexual assaults from happening will help protect people from becoming victims of sexual assault.

CHAPTER FOUR: DO I HAVE TO ASK?

Remember this

- ◆ Sexual Assault = Sexual Contact without CONSENT!
- ◆ Always get consent: Always ask!
- ◆ Be responsible for your actions.
- ◆ Think, "I want to ask."

Try this

Create two sets of posters. In the first set, teach people how sexual assault affects everyone. In the second set, show people how respecting their dates results in fun and healthy relationships. Be creative. Get permission to place the posters in local schools or colleges.

Bonus *(Chapter 4)*

 Strictly Students: Learn 2 ways to get students at your school WANTING to *"Ask First"* at www.mayikissyou.com/students.

 Parents Pointers: Help your child understand the dangers of dating and sexual assault at www.mayikissyou.com/parents.

 Teachers Tool: Discus the *"Long Term"* effect at www.mayikissyou.com/educators.

FIVE

You Can't Know
But You Can Help

Do you know the pain and trauma caused by a sexual assault? The emotional pain can be unthinkable. Understanding the trauma of a sexual assault can help each of us see the need to change the current "status quo" of dating. Sexual assault is considered to be the most devastating crime a person can survive.

Males and females have differing realities of sexual assault. Why? More women are victims of sexual assault than men. Through a friend, a loved one, or personal experience, more women have seen the pain sexual assault causes. In addition, many women have experienced nightmares of being sexually assaulted.

When a woman dates a man, she may be thinking about the potential danger he presents to her. She knows the man is probably physically stronger. Consequently, his physical being can be a weapon used against her. In addition to the man's body being a weapon, sex and sex acts are weapons he might use against her.

When previously comparing robbery to sexual assault, we showed why the comparison is not fair to an assault victim. Some people would say the comparison is not fair because the thief possessed a gun, which creates a more severe threat of danger. However, the man on a date possesses the weapon of potentially forcing his body and sexual acts onto a woman against her will. He could violently penetrate the most private parts of her body with his body or with an object.

Males have always had more of a struggle in understanding how disgusting and horrific sexual assault is for someone. Most males do not think they could ever be in a situation where they could be the victim. Not having the fear of being sexually assaulted may cause men to have difficulty relating to the trauma of sexual assault.

The one image of sexual assault men do find disturbing is male-on-male sexual assaults. When you tell the average guy to imagine a man raping a man, his face will cringe as he says "disgusting." If this image disgusts you, then picture this "disgusting" image of sexual assault every time you hear about a sexual assault victim, male or female.

When I make this statement to audiences, some men and women respond, "That is gross, because a man raping a man is not natural. I mean, you are talking about two guys." Are these people trying to say a woman being sexually assaulted by a man is natural? No act of sexual assault is natural!

Comprehending the pain and suffering caused by sexual assault helps us understand how horrific and unnatural this crime is. Only a victim or survivor can tell you what being sexually assaulted is like. As I have traveled the country, I have met thousands of sexual assault victims and survivors. I can share with you the anguish I have seen and experienced in talking with them, but I cannot tell you what it is like to be sexually assaulted.

How about this?

How can you learn more about the trauma a sexual assault survivor experiences? Contact a local rape crisis center or your state coalition against sexual assault. Find out the next time a program is being presented by a sexual assault survivor. Attend the program. Listen closely to the lessons the survivor will share with you. If you are in school, work with your school to invite a survivor to come and speak.

Victims and survivors will tell you how this crime can destroy your ability to feel safe. In almost every case, the assailant is a person the victim knows. What if your assailant lives near you or goes to the same school you attend? Imagine going to class and having to sit in the same room as the person who sexually assaulted you. Victims often want to drop out of school or transfer because of the fear of being near their assailant.

Before being assaulted, you take for granted going out and having fun. After being assaulted, you might look at every person and wonder if you are safe. If someone you know can hurt you so badly, what might other people do to you? How can you trust anyone?

Thoughts of being intimate and having healthy sexual relations are usually very positive thoughts. Once you have been assaulted,

41

your mind can have a very different view. You can be scared and frightened of what might happen during a moment of intimacy. You question if the person you are with could also behave like your assailant.

If you knew your assailant, your mind hasn't forgotten the trust you put in the person. Due to this memory, your mind can find it very difficult to trust anyone in any intimate situation. Why does the mind not forget? Your mind is very powerful and wants to protect you from any potential harm. By keeping the negative images in front of you, your mind is trying to remind you of what could happen to you.

After a sexual assault, you are likely to be in a "sexual" situation at some point in your life again. Hence, your mind faces the memories of the assault over and over. For some people, their mind will take the memory out of their immediate recall. These suppressed memories can continue to build up inside the person's mind leading to an emotional breakdown later in life.

HELP!

Due to the danger of an emotional breakdown, professional counseling for sexual assault victims is extremely important. Working with a professional counselor can help bring meaningful and lifesaving results to a victim. Without an outlet for victims to discuss their trauma and emotions, their feelings will build up inside of them. The stress from the buildup can be both mentally and physically damaging to that person.

Working with a professional can help a victim through the transition from victim to becoming a survivor. *A survivor is a victim who has learned how to cope with the trauma and lead a productive and fulfilled life.*

Unfortunately, most victims do not ever get professional help. Victims do not seek out help for two main reasons:

1. False stigma associated with counseling

When thinking of getting help through a counselor, people sometimes have a reaction of, "I am not sick or crazy. I do not need a counselor." Seeing a counselor does not mean you are sick, crazy, or less of a person. Counseling is an outstanding resource for victims.

A counselor is like a coach. Why does every great athlete in the world have a coach? The coach can tell athletes components of their game that the athletes cannot see while they are playing. A counselor can help you see what is happening in your life. A counselor can help you deal with your emotions and thoughts. A counselor can help improve your life.

2. Privacy

Victims may fear what they say to a counselor could be used against them or reported to the authorities. Young victims fear their parents will be notified or their peers will find out.

Rape crisis centers have been created across the world to solve these concerns for victims. Rape crisis centers provide confidential counseling to survivors of sexual assault. You can call a center and talk to a professional without fear of your privacy being violated.

Can privacy laws change? Yes. If you are not sure of the law in your state, just ask. When you call a rape crisis center, ask the professional if your conversations are confidential. The laws can be different for minors and adults. If you are under the age of 18, tell the person that you are a minor to ensure that the professional is giving you the correct legal information for your situation.

> *To find the rape crisis center closest to you, use the Internet and type in* www.DateSafeProject.org. *Click on the "Survivors" section of the website. You will find a link to all of the state coalitions against sexual assault. Your state coalition can tell you the closest location of a rape crisis center. Many college campuses provide their own counseling services at the campus health center.*

In addition to rape crisis centers, you can look up rape crisis lines, which are phone services staffed with trained personnel to help rape victims through their trauma. If the victim was recently assaulted, this is a great starting point. The day or night of an assault is an unbelievably emotional and stressful time for the victim. *Let the professionals help.* Call a rape crisis line or a rape crisis center. The services are often provided by the same agency.

Seeking medical treatment after a sexual assault can be critical to the life of the victim. An assault can expose a victim to pregnancy, infections, and sexually transmitted diseases such as HIV. Medical professionals can help manage these risks. If the victim ever decides to report the assault, the physical evidence can be vital to the criminal case. Evidence collection is usually offered twenty-four hours a day in emergency rooms.

If you have a friend who is a victim of sexual assault, do you force the victim into counseling or into reporting the crime? No. Your friend's perpetrator already forced your friend into something he or she did not want to do. The last thing you want to do to a friend is act like the assailant. Highly encourage, but do not force, your friend to get counseling and to report the crime. Provide the proper information so that your friend can take control and make his/her own informed decisions.

If the victim is hesitant, encourage him/her to call a rape crisis line to talk with a professional. The professionals know how to handle these situations. Explain the benefits of talking with a professional. Offer to go with your friend to a counseling center and to the authorities. Never force counseling. Never force your friend to file a criminal report. Always respect the victim's decisions.

How about this?

Go on the Internet and do research under rape crisis centers and sexual assault coalitions. Visit as many of these sites as possible and collect specific information on how these services can help a victim/survivor. With this knowledge, you will be better prepared to help a victim.

Blaming the Victim

Would you know if a friend or family member was the victim of a sexual assault? No, not normally. Most victims do not talk openly about their assaults—not even to close family and friends. The reason for this secrecy is because our society has a history of treating sexual assault victims poorly.

You can find numerous examples of victims being blamed for being sexually assaulted. The comments in italics below are just a few statements victims have heard people say. Each statement is followed by reasons why the comment is wrong:

"She asked for it."

Impossible. You cannot ask to be assaulted. An assault is without consent!

"That is what happens when you act like a tease."

You have the right to set your own personal standards on how far you feel comfortable going in sexual activity with another person. You always deserve to have your standards respected.

"You can't be getting it on with someone and then stop."

You always have the right to stop. If you say, "Yes" and then change your mind, you have the right to stop in the middle of whatever you are doing.

When a crime takes place, the criminal is at fault. The criminal took the criminal action, not the victim. Our society does not blame the victim in any other crime. We have no excuses for trying to blame the victim of a sexual assault.

Imagine being sexually assaulted and then hearing someone blame you for the assault. Imagine if the person blaming you was a family member or a friend. Would you want to continue talking about the assault? Blaming the victim is a major cause of victims not speaking out about their assaults and not reporting the assaults to the authorities.

How about this?

In schools and on college campuses, how do students react to hearing about a sexual assault? Do they blame the assailant or the victim? Try to think of reasons people try to blame a victim. Then, find the fault in the reasoning. As we have learned, a victim cannot ask to be assaulted and can never be blamed for being assaulted.

Example

What if the assailant is popular and well liked? Who will people blame? People might blame the victim because they don't want to believe a "good" guy could assault someone.

Supporting Victims/Survivors

How have you reacted when you heard about a sexual assault case? From the comments that you made, will a survivor think you are going to be supportive? Starting today, say the right words. Talk to everyone you care about and share the following message (referred to as "Opening the Door" for survivors):

"If anyone ever has or ever does sexually touch you against your will or without your consent, I am always here for you. Always."

Avoid adding statements such as, "If anyone ever does anything to you, I'll kill him." Comments of retaliation or violence will often scare the survivor from telling anyone want happened. Focus the conversation solely on supporting the survivor.

47

Why is it important to begin to tell everyone you can within the next few hours and days? You never know when someone has been or will be sexually assaulted. If a person hears you "Opening the Door" and is sexually assaulted months later, the survivor is likely to remember that you are a safe outlet. Or, if the person had been sexually assaulted in the past, he or she may see you as the one person who will be helpful and understanding.

Now that you have opened the door for a survivor, what do you say when someone tells you he or she was sexually assaulted? Many people mistakenly respond by saying, "I'm sorry" which survivors frequently feel is a statement of pity. Instead, show respect and admiration for the survivor by saying,

"Thank you for sharing with me. As a survivor, you are clearly a strong and courageous person. What can I do to help?"

Let the survivor decide what to discuss. Listen closely. From earlier in this chapter, you know the many options available to survivors. When appropriate, share those options. When "Opening the Door" for a survivor, you have the opportunity to make a positive impact on the life of another person.

Changing through Engaging

Do you know how to help change society's approach to victims of sexual assault? Do you notice how people negatively talk about what the victim "did" in a sexual assault case? Any time you hear a person acting in a disrespectful manner to a victim, approach that person. Engage the person in conversation. Do not attack the person for their comments. When verbally attacked, people attack back. You want to open the person's mind, not close it. Ask the person why they have the beliefs they are expressing. After listening, help them understand the fault in their reasoning. Under no circumstances is a victim at fault for being sexually assaulted.

Taking the time to educate one person can change the lives of many!

CHAPTER FIVE: YOU CAN'T KNOW

Remember this

- ◆ Sexual assault is unnatural.
- ◆ Sexual assault is devastating.
- ◆ Only the assailant can be guilty.
- ◆ Start "Opening the Door" for family and friends.
- ◆ Respect a victim's decisions.
- ◆ Counseling is essential and wonderful!
- ◆ Rape crisis centers provide privacy.
- ◆ Take time to educate others.

Try this

Donate your time to a local rape crisis center.

Bonus *(Chapter 5)*

 Strictly Students: The *"3 in 3 RULE."* Get it at
www.mayikissyou.com/students.

 Parents Pointers: Learn why your teenager having
a Strong Sexual Standard is essential at
www.mayikissyou.com/parents.

 Teachers Tool: The *"Blame Game"* is at
www.mayikissyou.com/educators.

SIX

Do You Understand?
The Crime, The Effect

Do you understand sexual assault? Do you comprehend the various forms of sexual assault? Sexual assault is a crime of power, of one person forcing his or her wants onto another person whether it be through physical violence or through mental manipulation.

> *For example, Kevin and Michelle are being intimate with each other. Kevin asks Michelle if she wants to have sex. She says, "No." He continues to try and persuade her into having sex. She says, "No." He goes back to kissing for a little while. He comes back to asking her if she wants to have sex. She says, "No." Now, she is getting scared. After continually telling Kevin "No," he is not giving up. Michelle is starting to worry about what he might do to her if she keeps saying "No." Kevin is not a big guy, but Michelle knows he is stronger than she is. He asks again. This time, he is pushing the issue even stronger. Out of fear he will become physically violent with her, Michelle says, "Yes."*

Michelle did not want to have sex with Kevin. Did she give consent? *No. Consent cannot be given under dire stress or a perceived threat of harm.*

Did Kevin put Michelle in a state of dire stress or a perceived threat of harm? Yes. His persistence and not listening to her wishes created a perceived threat of violence. His attempts to change Michelle's mind were manipulation. His never-ending efforts became a form of coercion that intimidated Michelle into saying "Yes." How else can you explain what he did? If he respected her, he would have stopped asking the first time she said "No." The threat of him acting out physically against Michelle scared her into saying "Yes."

Repeated attempts at sexual intimacy are common in relationships. When most people hear "No," do they completely give up on getting the person to engage in the sexual activity? No. People try to convince the partner why he/she "should." Excuses such as, "If you loved me," "If you cared about me," and "It will be fun" are a few of the many lines people use on a daily basis.

The other subtle form of manipulation is the diversionary tactic. When a person hears "No," he or she goes back to doing a more comfortable act of intimacy until trying again later on (similar to Kevin in the previous story). For example, Kevin wants to have sex, but Michelle says no. What does Kevin do? Kevin gives Michelle a backrub. As Michelle is enjoying the backrub, Kevin moves his hands into more sexual positions. After a certain period of time, he brings up having sex with Michelle again. She again says, "No." He returns to giving a backrub and the cycle continues.

Are you capable of being manipulative during intimacy? If so, make an effort to catch yourself before you disrespect the wishes of another person. If someone wants sexual intimacy, the person will say "Yes" the first time you ask. Trying to manipulate your partner into changing a decision of intimacy is a form of coercion.

Various forms of coercion are used against victims. Child molesters prey on young children's minds and bodies to convince a child that the perpetrator's perverse sexual acts are normal and healthy. People of lowered mental capacity have been sexually assaulted by trusted authority figures. We have seen teachers, coaches, and religious figures take advantage of their power to persuade minors into sexual situations.

Across the country, age laws exist to PROTECT minors from these forms of sexual assaults. However, teenagers often question the laws defining age and sexual activity. Many teenagers feel the law takes away their right to make choices. In reality, the law gives the minor more rights by helping protect the young person from criminals and individuals with wrongful intentions.

Why does a minor need protection? The 20-year-old man trying to be sexually involved with a 14-year-old girl can have an advantage over her. Through the experience of his age, he can know how to manipulate a younger person. Manipulating the mind of a minor for sexual gain is a crime. Here is an example of coercion.

A male is dating a female. He knows she has very low self-esteem. He knows she bases her own self-worth on that relationship. He believes if he stops dating her, she will become depressed and feel no self-worth.

53

As he tries to be intimate with her, she is not ready. She tells him, "No." He says, "You want to be my girlfriend? Then you're going to do this with me. Otherwise, I am not going out with you. If I dump you, no one is going to get near you. Not after what I tell them. You will be worthless. I am the one person who understands you and who will treat you right. All you have to do is do this with me and everything will be okay."

The man is knowingly manipulating the woman according to her greatest fears. He is emotionally tearing her down. Once she is emotionally weakened, he uses intimacy as his tool to build a false sense of self-worth for her.

Unfortunately, this scenario happens. If you know someone who will do anything with his/her partner just to stop the partner from breaking up, talk to the person. Help the person realize how valuable he/she is WITHOUT needing the dating partner. Help the person learn that people who care about you will never treat you so horribly. Call a crisis line to get advice on how to help this person get out of a manipulative relationship.

How about this?

Write down every "line" or excuse you can create that a person would use to manipulate a date into becoming sexually intimate. Then explain how the logic is flawed for each "line" or excuse.

Example No. 1

A female says to her male date, "Don't you think I'm attractive? If you found me attractive, you would want to do this with me."

Example No. 2

A male says to his longtime girlfriend, "We have been dating over six months. This is only natural. If you loved me, you would do this."

Physical violence is the form of sexual assault most people imagine when they hear of a "rape." You think of a man jumping out from an alley or inside a park to physically force a woman to the ground.

A "gang rape" is a physically violent assault perpetrated by multiple assailants. Gang rapes can happen at parties, night clubs, on the street, or in a person's home. You have read the trauma associated with an assault. In the case of "gang rape," the trauma is multiplied.

Have you noticed you rarely see the word "rape" in this book? "Rape" is seldom the correct legal term for this awful crime. Most states use the words "sexual assault" to define sexual contact without consent.

Family & Friends

All forms of sexual assault are damaging. In every case, the victim is the first person needing support. Who else needs help? The family and friends of the victim need help. Family and friends experience difficult emotions and unbelievable feelings of confusion.

I was in college when sexual assault changed my life and my family's life forever. A note was taped to my door. The note said

"Call Home IMMEDIATELY!" When I called, my mom answered and she said, "Mike, I have some bad news. Cheri has been raped." My sister, Cheri, had been raped! This could not be happening. I just started crying.

I wanted to kill the person who did this to my sister. Yes, I mean kill. I am telling you because you deserve to know the anger and rage sexual assault causes. More importantly, know it is normal to feel this way after a loved one has been assaulted. Did I act on my feelings? No! No one should. If I sought out revenge, I would have committed a crime and landed in jail. I would have made matters worse for everyone, especially for Cheri.

Within one year of my sister's assault, I went from being an honors student in college to almost being expelled for bad grades. I went from knowing exactly what I wanted in life to completely questioning everything in life. I searched for security and stability and found myself unstable and insecure.

How does this confusion happen? You never imagine this horrific crime happening to a loved one, and suddenly it does. You are shocked. You become overwhelmed with questions of, "How could this happen?" The fact my sister's assailant was going to prison for a long time did not matter to me. You still have anger and rage building up inside you. You feel guilty for not protecting your loved one.

All of my feelings and confusion were normal for the family member or friend of a sexual assault victim. I felt like I had no place to turn for help. If you are affected by another person's assault, get counseling. Parents, siblings, and affected friends of an assault victim need a professional to help teach them how to cope with this trauma.

How did my sister's being sexually assaulted change my perception of a rapist and the issue of sexual assault? When her assailant was being charged, I began learning about sexual assault laws. The law stated sexual assault is sexual contact without consent. Without consent? Even back then, I knew the only way you could definitely have consent was to ask.

I had never asked a woman before I kissed her. All of a sudden, I was looking at myself and saying, "Who am I to want to kill this rapist?" If I did anything with one of my dates and she didn't want it, I was similar to a rapist. I might have put a woman into an unwanted and nonconsensual situation.

Suddenly, the issue of sexual assault was not just about my sister being assaulted. My past was making me question my values and belief system. I wanted to make a change to ensure I never acted with disrespect toward a woman. After hearing Joseph Weinberg, a sexual assault activist, give a presentation on my college campus, I realized I could make a difference. I could make a difference in my life and the life of others.

I began researching the issue of sexual assault awareness. One of the first lessons I learned is that a sexual assault is a sexual assault. What do I mean? Whether your boyfriend forced sexual intercourse against your will or a stranger raped you in a parking lot, the trauma is horrific and the crime is a sexual assault.

I do not share the specifics of my sister's rape with audiences. No person needs to hear the details of a sexual assault. The mere thought of the rape should be disgusting without hearing the details of the horror.

How about this?

How can you help family and friends learn more about sexual assault awareness? Talk to your family and friends about healthy dating and sexual assault. The more people are aware, the more they have the opportunity to protect and help each other. Ask questions that will provoke conversation.

Example

Have you ever been uncomfortable on a date? Did you ever feel like someone took advantage of you on a date? Have you ever felt like you shouldn't have tried what you did with your date?

While having this conversation, do not overly pry into a person's privacy. If a person has been assaulted, he or she may not want to talk about the assault in front of other people.

Each Victim/Survivor Is Unique

The biggest mistake we can make in treating sexual assault victims/survivors is looking down on them with pity. Some people have difficulty looking face to face at a sexual assault victim. Do not have pity. Have understanding. Show respect for the courage and strength the person has in being able to recover from this trauma.

Society throws victims/survivors into one blanket stereotype. Ask people to describe the "typical" personality of a sexual assault victim, and they will use words like "quiet" and "scared." While some victims live the rest of their lives quiet and scared, many victims will live amazing lives. They will be inspirations to everyone they know. They will teach you that despite the worst crime being perpetrated against you, you can be a success in life.

The day I received the call about my sister being raped, I talked with her on the telephone. The first words from Cheri's mouth were, "How are you doing, Mike? Are you okay?" Am I okay? How could she be worried about me? A man had raped her just hours earlier and she was worried about me? Do you see where I get my inspiration from? Open your eyes and your heart, and look around. You will have the chance to be inspired by survivors all around you.

Society's Hidden Problem

Do you understand why sexual assault is difficult for our society to deal with? We have millions of victims and survivors. Those millions of victims and survivors have families and friends. Yet, few people are getting help. When you don't get help, you don't want to talk about the pain and/or the assault. The result is a culture full of hurting people from a crime that no one wants to discuss.

You can help change our culture. You can help people see the importance of this issue. You can help reduce the number of sexual assaults happening in the world. How? Get involved. Open up conversations with your family and friends. Challenge everyone to evaluate their beliefs on dating and sexual assault.

CHAPTER SIX: DO YOU UNDERSTAND?

Remember this

- ◆ Coercion is a form of sexual assault.
- ◆ All sexual assaults are horrific!
- ◆ Family & friends need counseling.
- ◆ Anyone can be a "rapist."
- ◆ Give victims and survivors respect!
- ◆ Meet a survivor & be inspired.

Try this

Next time you are with a friend or a group of friends, ask everyone what they think is the best way to date. Ask them to describe what they think about sexual assault. Could it happen to them? Could anyone they know commit this crime? Open their minds and their hearts to create change.

Bonus

 Strictly Students: Could someone pressure or coerce you? Find out at www.mayikissyou.com/students.

 Parents Pointers: You tell your teenagers the WAIT is worth it. As a parent, are you waiting? Go to www.mayikissyou.com/parents.

 Teachers Tool: What about the survivor in your classroom? Go to www.mayikissyou.com/educators.

SEVEN

Are You Aware?
Your Mind & Body

To help reduce the likelihood of you or someone you know being affected by sexual assault, develop an acute awareness for the issues concerning sexual assault.

Sexual Assault Awareness

The root word "aware" defines the concept of awareness. By being more aware, each of us can help ourselves and those around us to see potentially dangerous situations. Awareness helps us keep our eyes and ears open for trouble—without assuming that we can always "prevent" an attack. The more aware each of us is, the less likely an attack can occur.

What about "prevention"? The word "prevention" is widely misused in educating people about sexual assault. The root word "prevent" implies you can prevent all sexual assaults from happening to you. You can't! There is no 100% way to "prevent" a sexual assault.

By using the word "prevention," people might assume the victim "could have prevented the assault if . . . "—thus, placing blame on the victim for not being able to stop the assault from occurring. We never want to blame the victim. For this reason, awareness is the correct word to use when discussing sexual assault.

Gender Stereotypes

Many stereotypes of sexual assault create dangerous societal beliefs. One of the biggest myths is that "sexual assault is a man forcing himself on a woman." The use of the word "woman" implies that sexual assault only happens to women. The use of the word "man" implies that men are always the perpetrators. While the majority of assaults do fall into this category, assaults occur every year that do not fit this profile. Thousands of males sexually assault males each year. Females assault females. Females can, and have, assaulted males.

Whether you are heterosexual or homosexual, sexual assault is a real risk. Did you know that same-gender sexual assaults (male-on-male and female-on-female) are often perpetrated by heterosexual individuals? Sexual attraction has nothing to do with the motivation behind sexual assault. The crime of sexual assault is a crime of power, of one person forcing his or her wants onto another person.

Hate crimes against homosexuals have involved heterosexuals sexually assaulting a homosexual individual. These repulsive crimes are the perfect example of how sexuality is used as the devastating weapon in a crime of sexual assault.

One of the reasons victims are afraid to speak out is the image our society has created for each gender. Blanket gender statements create tremendous suffering. Some people in our society try to place blame on the victim for not acting like their gender stereotype.

"A real lady would never allow herself to be in that situation."

Are all women supposed to live according to one person's standard? No. Unfortunately, our society has been known to imply that women should live their lives a specific way. Think of the wording used in the comment about "a real lady." Do some women fit the profile of being "a fake lady?" Of course not. Each woman is her own being.

What harm is done by using the words "would never allow"? If you are a victim and you hear this statement, you could ask yourself if you "allowed" the assault to happen. Asking such a question can begin to build guilt inside you for the actions of your assailant. No victim deserves this extra burden of guilt to overcome.

"The guy is gay if he let another guy rape him."

Accusing a male victim of being "gay" is irresponsible. Saying anyone "let" an assault happen is an oxymoron. Sexual assault is a crime against your will. Millions of males have been sexually assaulted—many as minors and others as adults. The attitude above tries to diminish the reality of the male being assaulted.

Our society knows males have been assaulted. Why don't we hear more male victims coming forward to share their tragedies? By making such careless and cruel comments, we are creating a repressive environment for male victims.

A victim is a victim—regardless of gender, race, ethnicity, appearance, or orientation.

63

Weapons of Self-Defense!

The most effective defense against sexual assault is awareness. By watching for signs of trouble, you are better equipped to react before the trouble begins. If you use every form of awareness and self-defense available, will you be completely safe from being sexually assaulted? No. You will help greatly reduce the odds of you being assaulted.

Listen for comments that indicate the other person is not respecting your wishes. Listen for someone trying to coerce and/or manipulate you into changing your mind. If you think your date is not showing you respect, end the date. Have some-one pick you up. Do not let a disrespectful person drive you home. By ending the date and being picked up, you lessen a potentially dangerous situation with this person.

How about this?

Have a group of people watch at least two dating shows on television this evening. During the shows, no one can talk to each other. Instead, write down each sign of disrespect you notice a person on the show exhibiting during the date. Include all forms of disrespect (both for their own being and toward their partners).

When the shows are done, share your observations with the other individuals who watched the shows. Count how many times all of you picked up the same signs of disrespect. Decide what the people on the television show could have done to show respect toward each other while still having fun on the date.

To help reduce the risk of being with an individual who does not care about treating you with respect, Alan Berkowitz, consultant and author, points out that it is important to consider the following guidelines:

◆ Avoid putting yourself in a vulnerable situation with someone who is not willing to treat you respectfully.

◆ Avoid spending time with anyone who wants to control what you do and how you spend your time.

◆ Be aware of your surroundings and have a plan for getting help or leaving if a situation should become dangerous.

◆ Don't be afraid to assert yourself physically and verbally, even at the risk of upsetting the other person. Research shows that women who resist are less likely to suffer harm when assaulted.

If you see a friend or someone you know in any of the above situations, please consider saying or doing something to express your concern to the person.

Body & Clothes

Your body and your clothes are fantastic forms of defense against an attack. A belt, a shoe, a key, your finger, and many other items on your being can seriously hurt an attacker. A course on self-defense is the best avenue for learning these skills.

Self-defense Devices

Self-defense mechanisms such as mace, whistles, blow horns, and special alarms are great options to possess for moments when danger is imminent or occurring. Call your local police department to ensure that the device you are carrying or are considering buying is legal. The handling of devices is essential to their effectiveness. Self-defense devices have been used against victims. Carefully read over the instructions to use and handle the device correctly and safely.

If you carry a self-defense device or if you are trained in how to fight back, do not fall into the trap of thinking you are safe. Attackers look for people who are not aware of their surroundings and situation. A person who is not paying attention is more vulnerable to an attack. Try to look for signs of trouble before they occur. Be alert. Constantly use your skills of awareness.

"Safety" Space

If someone tries to make a move on you without asking, immediately create a physical space between the two of you. This space is called your "safety" space. Separate yourself from the person. If you are sitting together on a date, move farther away from the person. The physical space between the two of you provides a safer environment for you. The "safety" space helps create a "stop sign" effect toward your date.

As you quickly create a physical space, speak with a strong voice to let the person know you do not want the intimate action he or she is trying. You can almost always begin turning someone down by saying, "Stop. I really appreciate that you are attracted to me, but . . . "

Explain how you do not get intimately involved with anyone until you are ready. Share how you expect your partner to talk with you about what he or she wants to do before trying it with you. Most people have never received an education on healthy dating. Provide an opportunity for this person to learn from you.

If the person tries to make a move on you in a disrespectful manner (trying to force you into a position or quickly moving upon you, etc.), scream "STOP! GET AWAY FROM ME!" as loudly as you can. While screaming, try to create your "safety" space. Do not worry about embarrassing the other person by your screaming. The person was not respecting you. Protect yourself!

Plan Ahead

Planning ahead can greatly prepare you for threatening situations. Think of every way a person can be sexually assaulted. Think of how you would try to defend yourself in each situation. Thinking of being assaulted is an unpleasant thought process. You may never need this knowledge. However, the one time you are in a dangerous situation, your planning could have a significant effect on your safety.

Decide your boundaries for intimacy before you begin dating or start in a relationship. Having set boundaries helps diminish the level of confusion you might feel when you experience feelings of attraction toward another person. By having set boundaries, you are less likely to be asking yourself, "Should I do this with my date?" By having your boundaries decided, you will know the answer to the question before the situation occurs. Training your mind is as important as training your body!

How about this?

Write down your dating and intimacy boundaries. Write why you believe in setting the standards you have chosen. Before you go on each date, read this list out loud to yourself. By hearing your own boundaries and the reasoning, you will place the boundaries at the forefront of your mind.

Example

I do not kiss someone on a first date for two reasons. First, I do not want to give my date the impression that dating me means you are guaranteed intimacy. Second, after only one date, I don't know you well enough to begin intimacy. If you like me for who I am, you will wait until I am completely comfortable with you.

Shock

By learning self-defense moves, utilizing proper devices, and being completely aware of your surroundings, you help increase the chance of protecting yourself. Since 100% prevention does not exist, you CAN still be sexually assaulted. When an assault happens, you do not know exactly what you will do or will be capable of. You could try to scream and have no sound come out of your mouth. The trauma of being assaulted can cause shock and disable your body's natural defense mechanisms (your muscles freeze, you lose your voice).

When a person asks a victim, "Why didn't you say 'No'?" or "Why didn't you kick him?", the person is assuming that reacting to an assault is a natural process. During a traumatic experience, the body and the mind can shut down. Shock can limit a victim's capacity for logical thought progression. Shock can limit your ability to physically react to your assailant. You cannot blame the victim or hold the victim accountable for his or her immediate reaction during this awful crime.

Responsible Change

You have the ability to inspire change in people by helping individuals see the need for respect. You can help people learn to admire victims and survivors. In doing so, be responsible in your words and actions. If you do not know about a specific element of sexual assault, do not answer. Refer the question to a source who can solve the dilemma. Once you open a person's mind or heart, give them a great book to read on the issue of sexual assault, relationships, and dating. (See the suggested reading list at the end of this book.)

Utilize all of the resources available. Be sure that your efforts to change people's views are producing positive results. Repetition is one of the most effective education tools. Periodically discuss healthy dating and sexual assault with family and friends.

CHAPTER SEVEN: ARE YOU AWARE?

Remember this

- ◆ 100% prevention does NOT exist.
- ◆ A victim is a victim.
- ◆ Awareness, body, & clothes can be used for self-defense.
- ◆ Be responsible in educating others.

Try this

Do searches on the Internet under "sexual assault awareness." Visit at least twenty different Internet sites and write down ten ideas, facts, or concepts you did not know. Education is a lifelong process.

Bonus

 Strictly Students: Find the #1 self-defense move at www.mayikissyou.com/students.

 Parents Pointers: Have FUN creating your child's safety space at www.mayikissyou.com/parents.

 Teachers Tool: Get the *"What is in here?"* exercise at www.mayikissyou.com/educators.

EIGHT

Your Next Date
What Are You Doing?

On a date, how can you make yourself more aware of potential danger and signs of trouble? First, always keep one special word at the forefront of your mind—RESPECT. Being aware on a date is simply watching for signs of disrespect. Make sure you always act with respect toward yourself and your dating partner.

Since sexual assault is an act of power, you want to watch for all types of power plays. Are you making the decisions together or is one person trying to decide everything? Below are a few choices you make in planning a date.

Groups

Going out with a group of friends for a first date can be good and bad. If the group is laid back and not interested in the results of your date, the group setting could be very positive. The two of you are less likely to have any expectations of intimacy in a group setting.

If the group you go out with is capable of encouraging the two of you to "hook up" or "get together," this group behavior would be a very disrespectful environment for the two of you. With peer pressure being applied, you are likely to be persuaded into lowering your standards. You might try harder for a "connection between the two of you" just to please the group.

How about this?

What are comments that friends and peers can make to pressure a couple into sexual intimacy? What will you say if someone makes these comments to you? Role play with a group of friends. Have everyone try to pressure you about being intimate with your date. Before responding, notice how this pressure makes you feel. What do you want to say? Then, decide what is the best and most respectful response to the pressure being put on you by your friends.

Example

Kevin is about to go on a date with Michelle. Before the date, he is talking with one of his friends, Julie. Julie says to Kevin, "Michelle is hot for you. You have to go after her tonight." What does Kevin want to say? Does he want to say, "Oh, yeah?" What should Kevin say to Julie? What if Kevin says, "Julie, I like Michelle a lot, but I am not going to assume she wants me. If I think you are right, I'll ask her. I am not out only to 'get some' from Michelle. I assume you don't want me to treat women that way, do you, Julie?"

Establish the Rule of Talking

How do you create an atmosphere of equal respect when you go on a date? Talk openly and honestly. Talking will help you learn if the other person respects you. Plus, talking helps you learn about the other person (likes, dislikes, quirks, etc.).

Create an atmosphere of conversation before you go on the date. If you are asking the other person out, let the person know you want them involved in the entire process of planning the date so you can ensure that the two of you have an awesome time. As you talk and decide what you are going to do together, you will be building a foundation for open conversation throughout the date.

Time of the Day

Go on a date in the early afternoon to avoid all issues of being in dark locations at the end of the date. If you go for a nice walk together during the day, you will be in broad daylight. When other people can see you, both people are less likely to "try" making a move on the other person in a disrespectful manner. Additionally, there is much more to do during the day (parks, miniature golf, athletic events, etc.).

Be Creative

Stay away from the typical "movie" date. Do you want to learn about your date? While watching a movie, how can you get to know each other? Watching a movie eliminates all opportunities to talk and learn what the other person is like.

Think of a fun and simple activity where you can talk together throughout the event. If you are interested in each other, you can pick the silliest activity and you will have a blast together. Even if you are both horrible at bowling, imagine how much fun you would have laughing together and talking as you bowled. Write down all of the creative activities you could do on a daytime date.

Meet Your Date

While you are in your date's car, who is in control of the vehicle? Your date is in control. Your date has more control over where you go. Meet the person at the exact location of the date. You will have no safety concerns relating to driving or getting home.

If you are at a date's house, your date has more control. When someone is in their own home, he/she is much more likely to feel comfortable taking risks. Risk is not a good factor for a date. Never set the date to occur at a house.

How about this?

What can you do on a date that costs little or no money and does not involve intimacy? Think of creative dating ideas that are healthy, fun, and inexpensive. Remove the financial stress of dating.

Example

Go on a picnic to the beach.

Stay Close to Home

If your date is taking place at a location not easy for you to get home from, what will you do if the date starts going bad? What will you do if you don't feel comfortable or enjoy being around your date? Do not travel long distances. Stay close to home.

Who Pays

Who pays for the date can imply who is in control. When one person pays, some people feel they "owe" their date a kiss (or more) for paying. You do not owe your date a kiss or any form of intimacy. Are you an object for sale? No. You are a priceless person.

When two people are equal, they only owe each other respect. Date a person you consider to be your equal. Treat all of your dates like equals and expect your date to treat you as an equal. To completely avoid this perception of control, split the costs! Sharing the expenses of the date eliminates this entire concern for "owing" sexual intimacy.

If you are the person who requested the date, most dates will expect you to pay. If you are paying for everything, then do not expect anything for your paying.

When you are the person asked out on the date, try to split the costs. Keep the power equal between both people. You can always pay your half or decide to share which elements each person is paying for. For instance, if one of you pays for the meal, then the other person will pay for the entertainment venue the two of you attend.

Female Perspective

Some females are concerned that if they offer to pay, they will offend their date. In a respectful manner, explain your reasoning for wanting to pay. Here is an example of a female offering to pay her half on a date:

"When I go on a date, I believe in treating you with total respect. Making you pay for everything is not respectful, and

it would be selfish on my part. Actually, I enjoy paying because it makes me feel like we are working more as a team. I hope this is okay, because I am looking forward to the date."

If your date is offended by this explanation, take this as a warning sign. You clearly showed him respect, and you nicely explained your reasoning. You even told him you are excited about going on the date. If he becomes stuck on doing things his way, you may have a reason to be concerned. He may be selfish or self-centered. Talk with him to learn why he does not agree with you or why he is not willing to compromise with you.

Male Perspective

Most males going on a date are used to the role of paying for everything. If you are the one being asked out, you do not want to offer to pay for everything in an overbearing fashion. Doing so will make you look like you are trying to take control. An example of a male offering to pay his half in a caring manner may sound like,

"Thank you for asking me out. Before we go out, I would like to make one offer. I know that the person who asks you out is normally the person who pays for everything, but I want us to be equals this evening. If you pay for everything, it is not fair to you, especially when I am having a great time being with you. Therefore, I would like to pay for my half of the date. If I don't contribute, I feel like I am being selfish. I hope my paying half is okay with you because I am looking forward to this date."

Even if your date turns your offer down to pay, she can tell you care about her and respect her. You have set a very positive and unique tone for the date.

No Pity Dates

One of the most uncaring actions you can take is to go on a Pity Date or to give someone a Pity Kiss.

A Pity Date is when you are not interested in the other person. You go on the date only because you do not want to hurt the person's feelings. A Pity Date is extremely disrespectful to the other person's feelings. You are setting your date up for failure. Have the courage to do the right thing. Tell the person you are not interested and stress how you appreciate their asking you out.

Giving your date a Pity Kiss is a disrespectful and dishonest act. If your date asks you for a kiss and you do not want to kiss the person, do not kiss the person! When you say "Yes," your date thinks you wanted the kiss. By saying "Yes," you are lying. Always be honest.

Saying "No" to Being Asked

If a person asks you for a kiss and you don't want to kiss, appreciate the respect being given to you by the person asking. Tell the person, "Thank you for asking. I am honored, but . . . " and then fill in the reason. Explain the reason in a caring fashion. If you are not attracted to the person, say, "I don't feel a connection between the two of us."

STOP the Kiss

You ask your date for a kiss or any intimate act. The person says "Yes" in a hesitant fashion (not sounding as though he or she wants to). What do you do? Tell your date, "If you are not comfortable, that is okay. The last thing I want is to make you feel uncomfortable. We don't have to." As pathetic as a Pity Kiss is, you don't want to be the recipient of one.

Hold on to Your Standards

Hold on to your standards at all times. If a date tries to convince you to do something you don't want to do, be strong in your statements. You are a "10," so demand the respect of a "10." Once you have set high standards for yourself, you never want to question or lower your standards.

CHAPTER EIGHT: YOUR NEXT DATE

Remember this

- ◆ Show RESPECT for yourself and your partner.
- ◆ No power plays allowed.
- ◆ Start talking BEFORE the date. Be honest at all times.
- ◆ Only act according to your standards.

Try this

Come up with more examples of how one person could try to control his or her date. Next, decide how to avoid or handle those situations.

Bonus

 Strictly Students: Discover 3 fun, low-cost dating ideas at www.mayikissyou.com/students.

 Parents Pointers: Find 2 powerful statements at www.mayikissyou.com/parents to share with your teenager as he or she leaves for a date.

 Teachers Tool: Get the *"No Way"* Activity at www.mayikissyou.com/educators.

NINE

What Influences You?
Stop & Notice

Before and during a date, what are you filling your mind with? Are you listening to all your friends who are giving you advice? Friends can share well-intentioned, but very misguided, suggestions such as the following:

- ◆ How to impress your date.
- ◆ How to play the dating game.

Impressing Your Date

Do not try to impress your dating partner. Trying to impress other people only causes misleading behavior from you. Be the same person you are when you are hanging out with friends. If someone is going to like you, you want the person to like YOU.

Why do people open their date's car door? They do it to impress the date. If you believed opening the car door for someone is how you treat people well or is being "nice," then you would open the car door for everyone (your family members, your friends, etc.). How many people still open the doors for their partners after ten years or even after just a few dates?

By acting differently, you are not being yourself. You are lowering yourself to playing a game. Respect yourself. Be proud of who you are.

Playing the Dating Game

In a game, you have two competitors going against each other. Both competitors are trying to win at the cost of the other competitor losing. A great competitor does everything to play directly against the opponent's weaknesses. Turning a date into a game is a bad decision.

You can turn the date into a game without even realizing it. Do you or your friends use any of the following phrases?

- "Did you hit on him?"
- "Did you score?"
- "Play your cards right and you'll get some."

These expressions are commonly used in our society. Each phrase shows disregard for another human being. The words are violent and without care ("hit," "score," "get some"). Your friends might say, "They are only words," but words are powerful and lasting.

Your mind remembers the last message you send it. When your mind hears the above messages, it subconsciously focuses on scoring and winning. One person focusing on winning and scoring creates a dangerous dating atmosphere for the person who is going to lose. Eliminate all comparisons to a game and create a FUN date for both of you.

How about this?

Write down every comparison between dating and a game. Write down how people use these comparisons in everyday conversation. Challenge the logic and common sense behind each comparison. Explain the dangers and contradictions in using each dating analogy.

Example

"Did you score?" On the date, is there a scoreboard behind you? Each time you get what you want, does the scoreboard change in your favor? What if you disrespect your partner? Does your score get lowered for violating the rules? Can you get banned for life?

Peer Pressure

Do you realize how much peer pressure can influence the minds of two people going on a date? Analyze the pre-date advice Kevin and Michelle get from their friends in the following example:

Kevin is hoping Michelle is really cool. He would love for the two of them to "get it on" later in the night. Michelle wants Kevin to like her and to find her attractive. She wants to get to know Kevin. She wants to know if he is really a great guy.

Kevin has friends telling him how to set up the date so she is melting in his hands and totally hot for him. Michelle has friends telling her what to wear and how to use body language to draw Kevin in. Kevin has buddies telling him to get Michelle a little drunk to "loosen her up." Michelle has friends telling her to make sure she doesn't appear to be too "easy." Kevin has guys telling him how to take control. Michelle is being told how to play the game of being submissive by letting him think he has control.

Does the scenario between Kevin and Michelle sound complicated or too simple? Think about two people you know who fit these profiles. Think about the people you know who have been on this exact date. The scenario between Kevin and Michelle happens every night of the week.

Did you notice how none of the friends were concerned about the dating partner's wants or needs? Did you see how the friends pushed their own goals onto Kevin and Michelle? Peers will assume you have the same standards as they do (moral, ethical, sexual, etc.). Even though you know you are different from each of your friends, you start to forget your true self. You start to focus on everything your friends are saying. Suddenly, you have new goals and strategies for the date. Your motivation for the date has centered on the messages your friends have left in your mind.

You might be saying to yourself, "I would never do that!" When your friends are giving you advice, you do not notice the mental shift taking place in your mind. Kevin and Michelle are not purposely saying to themselves, "Forget what I was thinking before I talked with my friends. I am going to be self-centered like my friends are saying." The mental shift happens in your subconscious.

To ensure that you do not allow this shift to occur in your mind, watch and listen for the peer pressure. Once you recognize negative influences, you have the ability to block these harmful thought patterns. Family members, co-workers, and teammates can all offer negative advice. Watch and listen for negative influences so you can make the choice to keep negatives out of your mind!

Alcohol & Drugs

What other influences can affect a date? Mixing alcohol or drugs into a dating situation is extremely dangerous! Alcohol and drugs change the chemistry of your mind. Once the chemistry in your mind is changed, you do not have the ability to think as soundly as you did when you were sober.

You will have difficulty making respectful choices. You will find yourself participating in behaviors you would not approve of when you were sober. You will struggle to know the difference between right and wrong. This change in your mental status makes you more susceptible to taking harmful actions against another person.

When consuming alcohol and drugs, you may take risks that put other people in danger. You may take risks that put you in danger. Your cloudy mental state leaves you unaware of danger or trouble approaching you. All of these results lead to an unhealthy dating atmosphere.

Imagine if you were drinking on a date. Toward the end of the evening, you bring your date back to your place. As the two of you are kissing, you feel a false sense of "confidence." You decide to "surprise" your date by making a very fast move toward touching him/her in a private area. After you begin the touching, your dating partner yells, "Stop! What are you doing? How dare you touch me like that?" You just sexually assaulted your date.

83

If you were sober, you know you would not have acted the way you did. However, you weren't sober and you assaulted your date. You can't reverse what you did. The fact you were intoxicated does not excuse your behavior. Why? *You* took the actions.

You can only apologize. What could you have done? Made the safe choice and stayed sober. The vast majority of reported sexual assaults involve the use of alcohol!

How about this?

What are reasons that friends use for drinking or using drugs on a date or at a party? Write as many reasons as you can think of. How can you counter this way of thinking with reasonable logic?

Example

"I can't relax on a date without a few drinks in me." If you can't have fun with your date without drinking, why are you going on the date with that person?

Being Taken Advantage of

Every weekend, sexual assaults are reported where a person wakes up from being passed out and finds someone on top of him/her engaged in a sexual act. Is this behavior revolting? Yes. The victim does not have control over his or her body and may not even be conscious. Yet someone else chooses to force sexual acts on the person. This disregard for another human is indefensible.

Do you know the scariest part? Lots of people engage in similar behavior. Have you ever heard a person say, "Get her a little drunk. It will help loosen her up"? The person is encouraging someone to take advantage of a dating partner.

If you are intimate with a person who is heavily intoxicated or high, you are acting without consent. A "Yes" response from a drunk or high person is not consent. A drunk or high person telling you, "I want to have sex with you" is not consenting. To give consent, the person must be of sound mind. When someone is heavily intoxicated or high, that person is not of sound mind and cannot give consent. When you know a person has been drinking or taking drugs, do not become sexually involved with the person!

People will ask, "But what if the person really wants me?" If a person truly "wants you," then the person will still "want you" the next day when he/she is sober! Show respect and wait.

If your date wants you to get intoxicated, ask yourself and your date, "Why?" A person who cares about you will not encourage you to become more vulnerable or to lose control of your decision-making capabilities.

Date Rape Drugs

The most dangerous drug is the one you do not know you have in your system. This can happen when someone intention-ally spikes your drink or food with a drug you cannot detect. Unfortunately, more undetectable drugs are becoming available to the general public. When these drugs are placed in a drink, they have no visual cues or odor. You have no idea you are being drugged. You could be drinking non-alcoholic beverages such as juice or soda and still be drugged.

Devices are being created to detect these drugs. For example, companies are creating cup holders and coasters that will show whether certain drugs are in your beverage. Are these devices reliable? Currently, the answer is unknown. Many rape crisis centers do not recommend these devices because few studies have proven their effectiveness.

When someone puts a date rape drug into another person's drink, he or she is committing multiple crimes against another person!

Parties & Entertainment Venues

At parties, entertainment venues, and concerts, more and more sexual assaults are being committed with the aid of date rape drugs. The rush from being around a bunch of people your age gives you a false sense of invincibility. When you are having tons of fun, you believe nothing can go wrong.

At these places, keep yourself alert and aware of your setting at all times. Do not put your beverage down or let someone else handle it. If you start to feel as if you're becoming intoxicated, take action! Get a trusted individual to take you home. Date rape drugs can kill! If you suspect having ingested one, consider seeking medical attention and ask a trusted individual to keep an eye on you.

Imagine your beverage as a priceless item that means everything to you, precious because it is going into your body. If a drug gets into your system, your life can be shattered. Be careful. Your life is priceless!

Mob Mentality

Gang rapes can occur at parties. How can multiple people convince themselves to sexually assault the same person? Mob mentality. Individually, if each of the assailants were alone with the victim on a date, he/she may not have tried to sexually assault the person. However, when the assailants got into a group setting, they acted according to the group's behavior.

Two, three, four, five, or more friends are encouraging each person to "do it." Each person is being cheered on to force sex upon the victim. The group might say, "Have fun with her. She isn't even going to notice." The group keeps egging each guy on. Gradually, several guys start to believe in the group's behaviors and actions. The old "everyone else is doing it, why not me?" philosophy starts to enter another guy's mind. In the end, he becomes an assailant. They sexually assault a female through the horrid act of a gang rape.

Arrogance

Why is arrogance being discussed in a section about drugs and alcohol? Arrogance can act like a "built-in drug." It makes you think everyone wants to do what you want to do. If you believe everyone wants what you want, you might try to take actions that affect another person without asking. If you have an arrogant friend, help the person see the need to make changes.

An arrogant person might say,

"I don't need to ask anyone for a kiss or anything else. Everyone wants to be with me."

You could respond nicely by saying,

"If everyone wants to be with you, then why are you afraid to ask before doing something with the person? If they want you, they will say 'Yes.' Are you afraid they are going to say 'No'? Are you afraid someone might actually not want to be with you? If you really believe what you are telling me—that everyone wants you—you'll ask next time."

Challenge yourself to help people see the faults in their thought processes. Do not be a bystander to unhealthy behaviors. Make a difference!

CHAPTER NINE: WHAT INFLUENCES YOU?

Remember this

- ◆ Be yourself! Stay away from the games.
- ◆ Be aware of peer pressure.
- ◆ Do not drink on a date.
- ◆ Protect yourself at parties.

Try this

Write down more ways friends can be bad influences on your dating life. Then decide how you are going to block out those negative influences.

Bonus

 Strictly Students: Get your *"Party Pact"* at www.mayikissyou.com/students.

 Parents Pointers: For your son or daughter, make sure you use the *"Pickup Plan"* at www.mayikissyou.com/parents.

 Teachers Tool: Discover the *"Heard - Seen - Done"* exercise at www.mayikissyou.com/educators.

TEN

Students of Life
School Is In

Are you a student of life? Are you constantly learning from the people around you? Each person's environment can contribute to his or her own views of dating, relationships, and respect for others. When chosen correctly, your words and actions can help build a more positive atmosphere for everyone.

Language

Are you aware of the impact your words have on others? Awareness is more than listening and paying attention to the people around you. Awareness includes listening and paying attention to what you personally say and do. Do you laugh at jokes based on disrespect or filled with double standards toward males and females? When hearing such a joke, what do you do? Instead of the joke being sexist, what if the joke was racist in nature? Would you act differently?

You walk into a room and see a group of people talking to each other. One person, Kevin, is telling everyone a joke.

You join the group. The joke is racist and in bad taste. Everyone around you is laughing, but you don't want to laugh. Instead, you smile to avoid feeling out of place. Since everyone is laughing, Kevin continues with the racist jokes. When everyone else laughs, you continue to smile after each joke.

Are you a racist? You didn't speak out. By smiling, you appeared to approve of the jokes. By doing so, you promoted racist thoughts and stereotypes. Are you saying, "It was just a joke"?

Sexual Harassment

Harmful jokes can create an atmosphere of fear and intimidation for people offended by the joke or attacked in the joke. While most people know racist jokes can be damaging and are disrespectful, many people consider sexist jokes to be "okay." A sexist joke is a joke that makes fun of gender (just like a racist joke makes fun of a race or races). Think of all the "blonde" jokes you have heard in your lifetime. The majority of sexist jokes are based around negative stereotypes toward women.

How can blonde jokes or other sexist jokes cause harm?

A blonde female goes to school. By the age of 15, she has heard thousands of "dumb blonde" jokes. Does this repetition affect her? Yes. Would it affect you? Here is a challenge for you:

As you are walking into school, your friend approaches you and says, "What has happened to you? Your looks have gone downhill." What would you think? When you walk by a mirror, would you take a second look at yourself to see if the person was right? Later that day, another friend says, "What are you eating or doing to yourself? You just don't look the same anymore." After this comment, how long do you stare in the mirror? Now, two friends have made comments to you. Do you start to question your appearance or your value? You only heard two comments, and you were affected to some degree.

Words can be brutal and damaging. Harassment can occur anywhere: in your home, at school, at work, on a team, and many other places. Harassment is making someone feel intimidated, fearful, or uncomfortable due to your words or actions.

How about this?

Write down every possible example you have seen of harassment at school, work, and home. Be sure to include harassing comments to, and from, both males and females.

Example No. 1

You were walking down the school hallway when you heard a group of females say to another female, "You're the one with the big ... (fill in the blank)." Can that comment make someone feel uncomfortable?

Example No. 2

At a high school, a group of seniors yell out to a younger guy, "When are you going to hit puberty? You look like a girl in the showers." How would the guy feel?

What does "actions" mean? If you wanted to intimidate someone, you would not need to talk. You could stare the person down. You could stalk a person. You could continually invade a person's personal space. A group of people could constantly block another person from trying to get somewhere.

During a class, a woman notices one of her classmates staring at a specific area of her body. In the hallway, she catches the same guy staring at her in the same place. When she leaves school late at night, she sees him over near her car. Does she have a legitimate reason to fear him? He never verbally said anything, but his actions caused her to be intimidated and uncomfortable.

You are accountable for your words *and* your actions. When you hear a sexist joke, how can you use that moment as a learning opportunity for the people around you? Combining a compliment with a question is the best way to open another person's mind. For example, as soon as Kevin tells the sexist joke, say, "Kevin, I need to talk to you for just a second. Can I talk with you away from the group for one moment?" You don't want to embarrass Kevin. Doing so will only lead him to becoming defensive. Once the two of you are away from the crowd, nicely ask, "You have always been good at making people laugh. I was just wondering why you felt the need to tell a sexist joke. What if the joke was about someone you really cared about?"

Help the person realize the consequences he/she is creating by telling sexist jokes or making sexist comments. The words and actions we choose help create the environment we live in. Build healthier gender relations by keeping the air free of wrongful language and insinuations.

Is speaking out easy? No, but making the right choices helps improve relations between both genders. Speak out against the "norm." Knowing that you have helped another person is both satisfying and fulfilling.

Bystander or Caring Person?

If you could stop a sexual assault from taking place, would you? Most people say, "I would never let someone else be sexually assaulted." Yet the same person is likely to watch a man at a party take a highly intoxicated woman back home with him. The same observer may stand idly by as a group of guys brag about how to "keep the beers coming to Michelle. If she keeps drinking, one of us is going to get some tonight."

When you hear a person talk with disrespect toward a dating partner or a person at a party, what do you do? If you saw a person trying to take advantage of another person, what would you do? What if the person was not your friend? Friend or not, do not be a bystander. Are you afraid of embarrassing yourself by speaking out? If someone treats another person with disrespect, do not concern yourself with the disrespectful person's image of you. Concern yourself with the danger another person is being placed in.

Imagine leaving a party and saying to your friend, "I'm worried about Michelle. She has been drinking a lot, and who knows what could happen to her." The next morning, you learn that Michelle was sexually assaulted at the party. How would you feel? The assault is not your fault. The assailant is at fault. Yet, maybe you could have helped stop the assault from happening to Michelle.

Sadly, this scenario happens every weekend and most often we won't realize it. Normally, you are not going to know that Michelle was sexually assaulted because Michelle is not likely to tell you.

How many assaults can you help stop from happening? Write down everything you can do to help stop sexual assaults from happening.

You are at a party with friends. You see a really intoxicated female with a guy trying to get her to go home with him. What do you do?

Go up to the guy and say, "Thanks for offering to take her home, but we will take care of her. It was very nice of you to offer, but we really need to get her home." By intervening, you helped protect your friend from being sexually assaulted. Friend or not, you can help protect a potential victim.

You live in an apartment complex. As you walk by an apartment, you hear someone inside another apartment say, "I am not in the mood. Please stop." What would you do? Do you keep walking? Do you wait a minute to see if the situation is dangerous? How would you know if someone were in danger? Would you knock loudly on the door to see how the people inside respond? What if no one responded?

Err on the side of safety. If no one answers, yell, "Are you okay in there?" Drawing attention to the room might help deter a person from further assaulting someone. But keep your own safety in mind at all times. Do not stand next to the door. In a worst case scenario, an assailant could come out and try to force you into the room. After you knock loudly on the door, create a large distance between you and the door. Yell from a distance. In addition to helping you stay safe, your yelling will be drawing more attention into the hallway. If need be, call the police.

Will you tell?

You are in college and live in a residence hall. The residence hall has a 12:00 a.m. curfew for having persons of the other gender leave the dorm rooms. Imagine you are a female student on an all-female floor. As you walk down the hall at 1:00 a.m., you hear a male voice coming from a room. Do you tell the R.A. (Residence Assistant) that a man is in one of the rooms?

Can the male present a danger to the females living or staying in the dorm? Yes. What if, on his way out of the building, he forces himself onto another woman? These types of sexual assaults have occurred on college campuses across the country. Inform an R.A. about the man inside the room. If you are afraid of someone learning you "told" the R.A., then ask the R.A. to not tell anyone that you were the person who reported the violation. By helping reduce the risk of a sexual assault, you are helping keep everyone in the residence hall safer. Curfews and "locked door" policies were created to protect students living on campus and in residence halls.

What is a "locked door" policy or law? On college campuses, entrance doors to the residence halls are locked to keep strangers and dangerous individuals out. Frequently, students prop the doors open to let someone inside the dorm without having to enter through the main entrance, for example, to sneak a boyfriend or girlfriend into their room.

Unfortunately, numerous sexual assaults happen each year when assailants sneak in through these propped-open doors. You can help protect yourself and your fellow students by respecting these important safety policies on campus.

So you just watched?

What if you did nothing as you watched a sexual assault or a gang rape occur? By doing nothing to stop or report an assault, you are helping enable the assailants in their crime. In some states, you can be charged as an accessory to the crime. What if you were the victim? Would you want someone to call for help? By calling the authorities, you can help protect another human being.

Friends Act Like Friends—The Buddy System

If you go to a party, a club, or an event, go with a group of friends. Create a "buddy system" where each person has at least one friend who promises to help keep an eye out for them. You make a commitment to take any means necessary to protect each other.

You only leave the party with your buddy. You do not let your buddy leave the party with a different person. This rule is the one policy friends break the most often. Do not break this rule. Do whatever it takes to make your buddy leave with you. If you have to scream at the person and embarrass yourself, do it. Friends take care of their friends.

One way to help each friend understand the importance of the buddy system is to have a buddy dinner. Invite all of the friends you want involved over for dinner and talk about protecting each other. Let people ask questions and listen to their comments. Explain why the "buddy system" is vitally important. Once everyone agrees, have everyone commit to the buddy system.

Both males and females can create buddy systems.

Discuss the dangers of leaving a party with someone. Once you get in a car or the two of you are alone, you have no one to watch out for you. If a person wants to be with you or get to know you, make the person call you. Let them ask you out for a date!

Discuss the importance of not letting an intoxicated person go home with anyone other than the people he/she arrived with. Likewise, do not let the intoxicated person bring a date home. Help your friends stay away from troublesome situations. If a friend wants to go out with a certain person at a party, have your friend get a phone number. By doing so, your friend can call the person the next day when both people are sober.

Double Standards

Why do many people "look down" on females who are sexually active, but not men? Double standards. Our society has a different set of rules for males and females. We praise men for the same acts we ridicule and disrespect women for. Men are applauded for having lots of sexual partners, whereas women are called "sluts."

Listen for people speaking with double standards. If you hear a comment like "The little slut slept with him," ask the person, "What makes her a slut?" The person will probably tell you, "She sleeps around." Point out the double standard by saying, "If the guy wanted to sleep with her, doesn't that make him a slut?"

Double standards have become ingrained in our society. You can hear someone talk about a female classmate by saying, "The little slut got an 'A' on her test." You will not hear someone talk about a male classmate by saying, "Did you hear he got an 'A'? What a little 'ho' he is." Neither the female nor the male comments make sense, yet our society accepts the comment sexually degrading the female. In your everyday conversations, listen for double standards. Hold males and females to equal standards.

How about this?

Write down every double standard you can think of for females. Then, try to find the opposite standard for males. Switch the "stereotypical" roles.

Example

Write all the negative names for women who are sexually assertive. Then, write all the negative names for men who are sexually assertive. "Slut," "ho," and "tramp," are just a few of the words people use about women who are sexually active. For men, what will you come up with? The words must be completely negative (just like the words for the females were).

Privacy

Respect other people's privacy and sexuality. Do not spread rumors about another person's sexuality or sexual behavior. Do not brag about your own sexual relationships. Bragging is a sign of arrogance and shows no respect for your partner. Talking about other people only leads to their reputations and images being damaged. Have respect for yourself and your partner.

Use Logic

When you hear people discussing sexual issues or stereotypes, apply logic to the conversation. Frequently, our society belittles individuals who choose to abstain from sexual activity. If you examine the logic of a person who chooses to abstain, you see a person with great inner strength. You see a person who has the discipline to say "No" to an attractive opportunity. The person acts with strength when most people act with weakness. Logic would tell us to respect this person for making a strong choice. Use logic.

You can make a difference in changing our society's view of sexual assault, victims, survivors, dating, communication, and respect by getting involved in your community. Join your state's coalition against sexual assault. Start an organization in a local school or on a college campus.

Start a Date Safe Club

You can call your organization "The Date Safe Club." Your motto can be **"Request Consent. Demand Respect."** Inspire males and females to work together to educate others. Ask professionals to present workshops. Produce a weekly or monthly cable access show on important issues concerning your organization's efforts to make a difference.

Here is a good startup list of people to invite:
- ◆ Your state coalition against sexual assault
- ◆ Health teachers and counselors
- ◆ Student peer educators from schools and colleges
- ◆ Local authorities
- ◆ Friends and peers
- ◆ General public—Send press releases to local newspapers and provide public announcements for schools.

To learn more about starting a local organization, visit www.DateSafeProject.org on the Internet. You will find posters, educational tools, articles, podcasts, and many more ideas to help you make a positive influence in your local community.

Pledge for Action

What about making a difference throughout the world? How often do you receive e-mails asking you to "forward this e-mail to at least 7 people and in 10 days you will receive . . ."? Those e-mails are typically hoaxes. What if you could send an e-mail that actually changed lives? The Pledge for Action encourages people to make a caring commitment to their friends, family, and peers.

How do you put the Pledge for Action into an e-mail and get people to sign it? Go to www.Pledge4Action.org on the Internet and follow the directions. Start creating change today.

Talking with Your Elders

"Times were different back in my day. Men always showed respect toward women."

Have you ever heard an elder make the above type of comment? Men respected women? Women couldn't vote for hundreds of years. On a date, men would choose and order their date's meal for the evening. He would decide what she was going to eat. These "old" ideas of respect were misguided. In reality, disrespect for women has been ingrained in our society for centuries. Today, you have the opportunity to help improve respect for women. Accept this task with vigor and pride.

PLEDGE FOR ACTION™

I, _____, pledge to do my best to help my family, friends, and peers in potentially dangerous situations in which drugs, alcohol, a violent person, or other threats to their safety and well-being are present. I will do this by having the focus and self-control necessary to remain aware of my surroundings, the wisdom to identify dangerous situations, and the courage to take action in confronting my friends when their judgment is impaired.

I recognize that these dangerous situations may arise at times when people feel safe and comfortable, such as at bars, parties (especially when alcohol is influencing the situation and a person is trying to "hook up" with another individual), or in the context of a romantic relationship. I realize that it may not always be easy to help people from harm in these situations, but by remaining watchful and showing care and concern, I may help to prevent a sexual assault from occurring.

I understand that the ONLY person responsible for a sexual assault is the person who engages in sexual contact without the consent of the other person. Through my own positive words, actions, and beliefs, I am taking the responsibility of helping to end sexual assault. I will share with people the importance of consent and the need to obtain consent with your partner by Asking First. I will treat all survivors of sexual assault with my respect and admiration. I will inform all of my family, friends, and peers that "If anyone ever has or ever does sexually touch you without your consent, I will fully support you. I will always be here for you. Always (from simply listening to helping you seek the proper support from professionals)!" During the next 24 hours, I will start putting this pledge into action by saying these words to at least 3 people.

Sexual assault is a horrific and traumatic crime. My active commitment to this project will help reduce the violence in my community and create a safer atmosphere for everyone.

Signature _____ *Date* _____

Think about what you do have in common with the older generation. Did they get nervous before a date? Were they worried about what their date was going to think about them? Did they wonder how the date was going to end? Everyone has experienced these feelings of dating anxiety.

Ask questions in a respectful manner. Talk without being overly blunt. Do not outwardly ask about very private and intimate moments. While you may be trying to learn from the older person's experiences, it will appear you are just trying to pry into their personal life to embarrass them.

Start by asking your elders simple questions like the following:

"How did you approach a date?"

"What do you think is the most important lesson to remember when dating?"

"If you could do it all over again, what would you change about the way you dated?"

Elders can provide you with fantastic life lessons to use in your dating life.

Fun

Dating and relationships are one of the few components in life where you can experience the wide range of emotion from fear to pure joy and happiness. Violence, disrespect, and pain do not belong on any date or in any relationship.

Each person can help change the atmosphere toward sexual assault in our culture. With the knowledge and understanding you have, you can challenge the harmful thoughts of others. You can engage individuals in conversations. You can bring the word "RESPECT" to the forefront of relationships. You can inspire admiration and compassion for victims/survivors. You can make dating healthier and more fun. You can help reduce the occurrence of sexual assault. By doing so, you can change the lives of many.

Be responsible.
Make a difference!

CHAPTER TEN: STUDENTS OF LIFE

Remember this

- Stop sexism from spreading.
- Listen for and eliminate harassment.
- Don't watch. Take action.
- Speak out to keep schools safe.
- Create a "buddy" system.
- Demolish double standards.
- Start a *Date Safe Club*.
- **Pledge for Action.**
- Connect with your elders & learn.
- Get involved.
- Make a difference!

Try this

Write down exactly what you are going to do to make a difference. There is only one rule. You must start taking the action today.

Bonus *(Chapter 10)*

 Strictly Students: Start making a difference with your friends TODAY. Go to: www.mayikissyou.com/students. Start a *"Date Safe Club"* at your school.

 Parents Pointers: Imagine having every parent teaching the right messages to their children. Your job would be MUCH easier. Give all your child's friends the chance to learn the messages in this book by bringing a sensational program to your school and community. Find out more at www.mayikissyou.com/parents.

 Teachers Tool: Keep the message going all year. Hear exactly what to say to your students when real cases break in the media, especially with all the celebrity news nowadays. Go to www.mayikissyou.com/educators.

NOTES

Suggested Reading

To see a complete list of resources visit <u>www.DateSafeProject.org.</u>

After Silence: Rape and My Journey Back. Nancy Venable Raine (Three Rivers Press, 1999).

Date Rape: A Hot Issue. Kathleen Winkler (NJ: Enslow Publishers, Inc., 1999).

Date Rape: The Secret Epidemic. Marcia Mobilia Boumil and Joel Friedman (FL: Health Communications, Inc., 1996).

[The] Date Rape Prevention Book: The Essential Guide for Girls and Women. Scott Lindquist (IL: Sourcebooks, Inc., 2000).

Dating Violence: Young Women in Danger. Barrie Levy (WA: Seal Press, 1991).

I Never Called It Rape. Robin Warshaw (NY: Harper & Row Publishers, 1988).

Lucky: A Memoir. Alice Sebold (Back Bay Books, 2002).

[The] Macho Paradox: Why Some Men Hurt Women and How All Men Can Help. Jackson Katz (Sourcebooks, Inc, 2006).

Man to Man: When Your Partner Says No—Pressured Sex & Date Rape. Scott Allen Johnson (VT: Safer Society Press, 1992).

Men and Rape: Theory, Research, and Prevention Programs in Higher Education. Alan Berkowitz (CA: Jossey-Bass Inc Publishing, 1994).

Men's Work: How to Stop the Violence That Tears Our Lives Apart. Paul Kivel (Hazelden Publishing & Educational Services, 1999).

[The] Other Side of Silence: Women Tell About Their Experiences with Date Rape. Christine Carter, Ed. (NH: Avocus Publishing, Inc., 1995).

Our Guys: The Glen Ridge Rape and the Secret Life of the Perfect Suburb. Bernard Lefkowitz (Vintage Books, 1998).

Sexual Assault in Context: Teaching College Men About Gender. Chris Kilmartin and Alan Berkowitz (FL: Learning Publications, 2000).

Sexual Coercion in Dating Relationships. E. Sandra Byers and Lucia F. O'Sullivan (NY: The Haworth Press, Inc., 1996).

Stopping Rape: A Challenge for Men. Russ Ervin Funk (New Society Publications, 1993).

Transforming a Rape Culture. Emilie Buchwald (Milkweed Editions, 1995).

Voices of Courage: Inspiration from Survivors of Sexual Assault. Mike Domitrz (WI: Awareness Publications, 2005).

When "I Love You" Turns Violent: Emotional and Physical Abuse in Dating Relationships. Scott A. Johnson (NJ: New Horizon Press, 1993).

When You Are the Partner of a Rape or Incest Survivor: A Workbook for You. Robert Barry Levine (Resource Publications, 1996).

[A] Woman Scorned: Acquaintance Rape and Trial. Peggy Reeves Sanday (NY: Doubleday, 1996).

About the Author

Mike Domitrz is an internationally renown speaker and a critically acclaimed author who has devoted his life to educating society about dating, communication, respect, consent, and sexual assault awareness.

After the devastation of his sister being sexually assaulted in 1989, Mike was determined to make a difference. While still in college, he created and designed his own interactive presentation,

Michael J. Domitrz

"Can I Kiss You? Dating, Communication, Respect, & Sexual Assault Awareness". His goal was to open the eyes of people toward this important societal issue.

His impact on audiences has made Mike one of the most sought-after presenters in schools, on college campuses, and at educational conferences.

In the past decade, Mike has become one of the leading authorities on consent, intimacy, and sexual assault awareness. He created "The Date Safe Project" to launch national initiatives and produce educational products to assist students, parents, educators, and survivors throughout the world (www.DateSafeProject.org).

Audiences have been asking Mike to put his ideas and concepts into a book that everyone could use. *May I Kiss You?* is the product of that demand.

To learn more about Mike visit www.DateSafeProject.org

Bring Mike to Speak

To schedule Mike for a keynote speech, assembly, convocation, seminar, workshop, convention, or training session, contact:

The Date Safe Project
Milwaukee, Wisconsin
(800) 329-9390

Mike will customize the entire program to fit the needs of your audience and your organization. When students, educators, administrators, counselors, and parents hear Mike speak, they stand together in praise of his message and his approach. He exposes the problem and then inspires people with simple solutions!

Visit Mike on the internet at:
www.DateSafeProject.org

E-mail: mike@datesafeproject.org

You Will Want to Read

Voices of Courage:
Inspiration from Survivors of Sexual Assault

Edited by Mike Domitrz

From tragedy to triumph, inspiring lessons unfold in this one-of-a-kind book by twelve survivors of sexual assault. An eye-opening journal of personal growth and recovery, *Voices of Courage* will forever change your perspective on life after a sexual assault. As you read the depth of the survivors' pain and share in their greatest moments of enlightenment, you will find yourself riveted with emotion.

Unlike reading most sexual assault books that focus only on the horror of rape, *Voices of Courage* will explore the optimism and hope that surviving sexual assault brings to many survivors' lives. You will be uplifted and inspired by the amazing strength and courage these twelve survivors live with on a daily basis. Order this book today for $16.95 at www.VoicesOfCourage.com.

AWARENESS PUBLICATIONS

P.O. Box 20906
Greenfield, WI 53220-0906

www.VoicesOfCourage.com

More Educational Products

Spread the important and powerful message of "Asking First" through educational materials produced by The Date Safe Project. From T-shirts to temporary tattoos, these items will help you to share this message with family, friends, and your entire community.

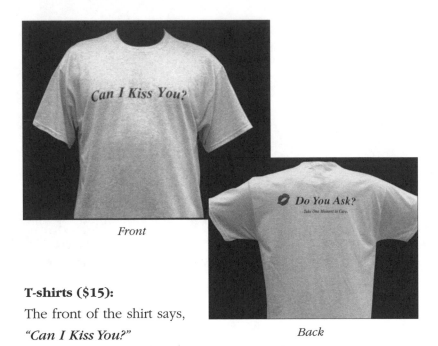

Front

Back

T-shirts ($15):
The front of the shirt says,
"Can I Kiss You?"

Back of the shirt says,
"Do You Ask? - Take One Moment to Care"

T-shirts ($15):

The front of the shirt says,
"Want Some Action?"

Back of the shirt says,
"Take the Pledge 4 Action"
  1. Respect Yourself
  2. Respect Your Partner
  3. Ask B4 You Act
  4. Respect the Answer

Front

Back

"HELP! My Teen is Dating"

Real Solutions to Tough Conversations

The ultimate DVD and book combo for parents of teenagers! Discover how to properly prepare your teenagers for the dangers of dating in today's sexual culture. In this 85 minute interactive DVD, you learn the keys to engaging your child in powerful and fun conversations on dating, intimacy, and sexual choices. Mike Domitrz uses humor and a straightforward approach to give each parent the 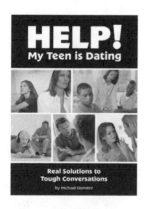 exact tools needed to vastly improve their child's decision-making on dates and in potential moments of intimacy. This video is so much fun and powerful that many teenagers actually love watching it WITH their parents! Get this fantastic package at www.HelpMyTeenIsDating.com

Buttons ($10 for 40 Buttons):
Buttons say, *"Can I Kiss You?"* and the next line says, *"Do you ask?"* Wear these fun buttons everywhere you go and watch how many people ask you to share the message.

Tattoos (200 for $25)
Each tattoo is 1.5 inches by 1.5 inches—great for students to wear on their cheeks, hands, arms, and other easily visible locations. (They wash right off!)

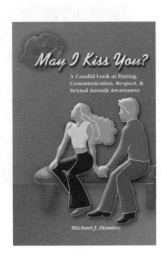

Pick Your Favorite Format
You can order *May I Kiss You?* in the following three formats:
- Paperback ($19.97)
- Audio Book on CD or download ($24.97)
- E-book, pdf file ($9.97)

All of these products may be ordered online at: www.DateSafeProject.org

The Date Safe Project, Inc

Join The Date Safe Project today! Be a part of a community where students, parents, educators, survivors, and the military are sharing innovative and helpful ideas to use in their own lives. Visit www.DateSafeProject.org right now to see what everyone is talking about.